FEEL SOMETHING:
HOW TO EMBRACE EMPATHY
AND BUILD TRUST WITH
YOUR AUDIENCE

FEEL SOMETHING:

HOW TO EMBRACE EMPATHY AND BUILD TRUST WITH YOUR AUDIENCE

PATRICK TIMMONS

NEW DEGREE PRESS
COPYRIGHT © 2021 PATRICK TIMMONS

FEEL SOMETHING:
HOW TO EMBRACE EMPATHY AND BUILD TRUST WITH YOUR AUDIENCE

ISBN   978-1-63730-424-2   *Paperback*
           978-1-63730-505-8   *Kindle Ebook*
           978-1-63730-506-5   *Ebook*

"I've learned that people will forget what you said, people will forget what you did, but people will never forget how you made them feel."

—MAYA ANGELOU

To those in my life who lift me up, support me, and believe in me.

To my incredible family: Mom, Dad, Kristin, and Brendan—your love is so strongly felt.

To my four grandparents—thank you for teaching me lessons to navigate the world.

To my whole family—thank you for giving me strength.

To my four beautiful nieces: Emery, Pepper, Teagan, and Marlo—thank you for bringing me so much joy.

To the true friends I have met over the years—I would not be who I am without you.

To the leaders who have inspired me along my career—thank you for helping me fall in love with learning about people.

To my readers—thank you for embracing empathy and making the world a better place.

TABLE OF CONTENTS

_____

EMPATHY, WHERE ARE YOU?

———

On November 7, 2020, the word "empathy" shined brightly on millions of devices in the United States as Joe Biden delivered his acceptance speech.

The year 2020 will go down in history as one of the most tension-filled in America. With a high-stakes presidential election, civic unrest, and a global pandemic, it was hard. It is still hard. On November 7, however, Joe Biden delivered his president-elect acceptance speech with the words "America Chose Empathy" beaming behind him. While empathy is used quite often as a buzzword, this action seemed to be very intentional. No matter what party you voted for during this election, it's clear that our country is divided. Right in half. Fifty-fifty. The United States of America feels like pure irony at this point—especially in the midst of a global pandemic killing thousands of people every day.

Division runs even deeper through pop culture, sports, entertainment, and more. For years people loved the tension of hating a sports team because they love another team. Music fans always claim that their favorite artist is superior to another major artist. This tension is strong and ever present. It is what our society eats, drinks, and breathes. I'm guilty of it, and I'm sure you are too.

So, how do we overcome this division?

It all comes to that word that beamed on November 7, 2020—Empathy.

In 2020, over 3.6 billion people were using social media worldwide, a number projected to increase to almost 4.41 billion in 2025 (Tankovska, 2021). Social networks are changing constantly and growing at an incredible speed. More than half of the people on Earth use social media (Kemp, 2021). Whole crowds are doing TikTok dances at clubs (don't ask, 2021). The exponential growth of social media affects us more than we realize, and psychologists are trying to determine how. The *International Journal of Mental Health Systems* published a study that focused on social media's effects on personality, our ability to evaluate risk, and development (Zyoud, Sweileh, and Awang, 2018). This research alludes to the fact that psychologists are concerned about the effect that social media has on these areas and that there are many unknowns.

Social media plays an increasing importance in our society. Companies need to slow down their use of it as a marketing tool and treat it like more of a way to connect with one another.

Division runs even deeper through pop culture, sports, entertainment, and more. For years people loved the tension of hating a sports team because they love another team. Music fans always claim that their favorite artist is superior to another major artist. This tension is strong and ever present. It is what our society eats, drinks, and breathes. I'm guilty of it, and I'm sure you are too.

Companies that understand that their brand plays a big role in the lives of their consumers from a psychological perspective and an entertainment perspective will win. But how do they tactfully do that? With empathy. By bringing humanity to their brand and showing deep passion for your customers. With that brand personality, they form meaningful connections with their audience.

A lot can improve when you think differently as a social manager to create a persona that is mission-driven. I wondered if this approach was unique and something all of us could learn from, and what I found has changed the way I see the future.

According to *Forbes*, "Employees who fall in love with their work experience higher productivity levels and engagement, and they express loyalty to the company as they remain longer, costing the organization less over time. Mission-driven workers are 54 percent more likely to stay for five years at a company and 30 percent more likely to grow into high performers than those who arrive at work with only their paycheck as the motivator" (Craig, 2018). It makes sense; if your company is mission-driven and shows empathy for others in the world, you'll have a better sense of purpose in your role.

The same goes for individuals. With the rise in social media and the focus on mission-driven companies, people have been focusing on branding themselves. This paradox of companies becoming more like humans and humans becoming more like companies creates an interesting playing field for the concept of what it means to be empathetic and who or what gets to practice empathy. If you don't embrace empathy and are not focused on a mission, or if you stray away from either, you run the risk of confronting cancel culture—a modern form

Companies that understand that their brand plays a big role in the lives of their consumers from a psychological perspective and an entertainment perspective will win. But how do they tactfully do that? With empathy. By bringing humanity to their brand and showing deep passion for your customers. With that brand personality, they form meaningful connections with their audience.

of ostracism in which someone is thrust out of social or professional circles, either online or offline. Why? Because people are empowered to make their voices heard on social media but also because social media "has been linked to higher levels of loneliness, envy, anxiety, depression, narcissism and decreased social skills." (Silva, 2017) Empathy, if fully embraced, is a strong remedy to the issues we see above.

Some people think empathy is a magic superpower that you can only have if you are born with it. This is not true.

NBC News reported that "research suggests that about 50 percent of our empathic capacities are genetically inherited and the rest we can learn, because empathy is not simply a matter of wiring...adversity can also lend itself to the development of an empathetic nature." (Manning-Schaffel, 2018). We all have the ability to learn empathy, embrace it, and act on it in our professional and personal lives.

The problem is that people do not believe it is possible for them to learn how to embrace empathy if they don't have that trait. And I'm here to prove them wrong.

Everyone is able to embrace empathy. Everyone is able to understand another person's point of view; however, it ain't no cake walk. This book is for marketers who are at the frontlines for their customers: social media managers, product marketing managers, sales professionals, customer marketing teams, chief marketing officers, and more.

As a professional marketer myself, I have worked in the marketing industry in pretty much every form possible. From my time in public relations to advertising, the music industry to user experience and tech, I have learned from countless experts in marketing, psychology, empathy, and more. In addition to my professional experience, I have always been an emotionally intelligent person (*hair flip*). I know when people are feeling certain emotions, and I know how to act on them. Empathy is an instinct for me both in and out of work.

Throughout this book I am going to highlight people who have similar experiences—those who use empathy in their professional and personal life to achieve success, value, and trust in order to create deep bonds with their customers and fans.

This book is for anyone who wants to focus more on the emotions of others and actually turn that focus into action. It is for those who hear the word empathy thrown around a lot and don't really know what empathy means or how to act on it. This book is for professionals who want to build lasting impact in their work with empathy. Social media managers, executives, and small business owners will all learn a ton from using empathy in a tactful way.

I am going to tell you stories from the greatest minds of our time. From the head of Google's Social Lab to Velveeta Cheese, philosophers to psychologists, a HubSpot employee to international speakers like Daniel Pink, Gary Vaynerchuk, Jamil Zaki, and more, you will learn how to apply empathy to your work daily. You will build trust with your audience, build your brand, and grow revenue.

Ready?

Let's do it.

CHAPTER-1

WE ALL THINK WE ARE RATIONAL, BUT...

My mom always shared Maya Angelou's famous quote, "I've learned that people will forget what you said, people will forget what you did, but people will never forget how you made them feel." In today's digital world that could not be more true. We are so constantly bombarded with noise, information, and marketing that it is near impossible to remember every message you scroll past on social media. However, if they do it right, you remember how those brands made you feel.

In March 2020, the world had the same feelings. Shock. Fear. Confusion. The global COVID-19 pandemic became strong, intense, and powerful.

At the time, I was starting my new position at my company, but it was from home. I went from video intern to social media intern, and in that transition period, the whole world went into lockdown.

I realized early on this was a shift.

This was a shift in how we all would work, live, and feel. I made sure to approach social media in that way.

People did not want to be sold to. Actually, they never really did. They wanted to feel safe. They wanted to feel heard. They wanted to feel some sense of normalcy, and as a marketer, I was one of the people who could help them do that.

I realized how I could use my superpower, empathy, in a meaningful way. I understood the importance of writing to people's emotions not just the "target demographic." By using language that involved them and made them the focus of the conversation, I was able to make the audience feel something.

I realized the power of marketing that focuses on emotions. I studied companies that do this on a regular basis. Then I created a new category—Empathy Marketing.

Let me tell you how I got there.

In the midst of the pandemic I decided to seek therapy to keep up with my mental health. I had always said that "everyone should have a therapist to stay in touch with their mental health," but I was just talking the talk. Finally, I decided a global pandemic might be a good opportunity to walk the walk.

I reached out to my sister-in-law down in Nashville because I knew she had an amazing therapist, and I wanted that. I needed someone I could trust.

Soon after I was talking to my therapist, Trey, weekly about my personal identity, life, the world, and how it all interacts.

The best part about Trey is that he knows therapy is a journey. He knows it is about evolving, not fixing. Trey utilizes an ancient tool called the Enneagram to understand people's personalities as well as study how it affects their lives,

People did not want to be sold to. Actually, they never really did. They wanted to feel safe. They wanted to feel heard. They wanted to feel some sense of normalcy, and as a marketer, I was one of the people who could help them do that.

motivations, interactions with others, and, ultimately, how they feel.

The tool is powerful, incredibly accurate, and comprehensive. With nine different archetypes, the Enneagram is able to depict a clear picture of the different types of people in this world.

Between the above experiences, something clicked.

Empathy and marketing seemed like the most obvious grouping in the world, yet no one has talked about it.

What if marketers could understand what makes people tick on an emotional level and use empathy to act on that through every phase of the buyer's journey? What makes certain people feel certain things?

Continue on this journey with me as we find the answers to those questions.

After the pandemic, marketers everywhere realized that empathy is not only important, but it is an essential part of their strategy. This book will help you create an empathy-integrated marketing strategy for you and your team to act on and to build trust with your audience at every step of the buyer's journey.

Most people have the ability to practice empathy, but the action takes practice. Let's get into it!

UNDERSTANDING EMPATHY

During the pandemic we were all home, secluded, and safer than ever. While COVID-19 cases were rising, flu activity was significantly lower compared to previous years (Ries, 2020).

Empathy and marketing seemed like the most obvious grouping in the world, yet no one has talked about it.

However, every time something happened in the world, we all felt the same emotions. The catastrophic numbers of deaths from COVID-19, the civil unrest, and more all invoked the same emotions in most of the world.

You may be wondering, is it possible the entire human race could feel empathetic toward one another at the same time?

Yes.

It is possible with work.

Empathy is engraved into our human nature, and it is something we have been experiencing since the beginning of time. Empathy has gone from blood ties to religious association ties and national identification ties, and now with technology, we can connect our empathy to a single biosphere.

What does that even mean? Let's walk through it.

Cave men and women only felt empathy toward people of their own blood. Their main goal was survival and anyone outside of their circle was a threat. However, according to *Wired*, "Most of our Neanderthal skeletons show some evidence of having been looked after for their injuries. And in the age of Neanderthals, you also start to see evidence of deliberate burials and funerary rites. That means a shared feeling" (Keim, 2010). This suggests that Neanderthals had a strong sense of compassion for those they lived with. They knew there was a shared feeling, and they knew how to act on it.

Jeremy Rifkin is a bestselling author of the book *The Empathic Civilization*. He breaks down the history of empathy and why it is so important. As time went on, the Neanderthals evolved, and survival wasn't the primary concern for the human race—religion was. If you were in the same religion, you felt empathy for those people. For the people who celebrated other religions, empathy was lacking. Unfortunately empathy across religions continues to be absent and results in hate.

Throughout the industrial revolution, nationalism became important for people, and many humans focused their empathy on others in their own country. According to Jeremy Adam Smith, the online editor of *Greater Good* magazine, "Patriotism helps tie us together within national borders, but there's a catch: It seems to diminish our ability to see the humanity in citizens of other nations." Smith argues that because of intense nationalism, "we feel forced to choose between country and humanity" (Smith, 2013).

Rifkin now argues that with technology, we can empathize across all of the boundaries above through—you guessed it—social media.

Rifkin mentions that "we have the technology to think viscerally as a family. When the earthquake in Haiti happened, within one hour Twitter was sharing the news, within two hours there were videos all over YouTube, and within three hours the entire human race went to Haiti in an empathetic embrace." This is true with many crises that humans experience today.

WHAT EMPATHY LOOKS LIKE TODAY

Think about COVID-19. During the pandemic "Social media consumption increased by 32 percent (US) and 44 percent (globally) of internet users in March 2020 alone" (MediaKix, 2020). At the onset of the pandemic, our gut instinct was to find community, empathy, and compassion on social media.

Think about the Black Lives Matter movement. In 2020, the Pew Research Center analyzed publicly available tweets: "As nationwide protests continue over police brutality and the death of George Floyd, the #BlackLivesMatter hashtag, which is often used in connection with police-related deaths of Black Americans, has been used roughly 47.8 million times on Twitter—an average of just under 3.7 million times per day—from May 26 to June 7" (Anderson, Barthel, Perrin, Vogels, 2020). Not only did we come together on social media to learn and stay up to date, but we came together to support a movement, enact change, and make voices heard.

The possibilities for empathy through technology have no limits, and it is powerful. Powerful enough to raise millions of dollars for people in need. Powerful enough to cause peaceful protests and, unfortunately, riots. Another Pew Research Center study found that "23 percent of users in the US say social media led them to change views on an issue" (Anderson, Barthel, Perrin, Vogels, 2020).

Rifkin mentions that empathy is not always focused on the positive. "Empathy is grounded in the acknowledgment of death and the celebration of life," he writes. "It's based on our frailties and our imperfections." Empathy embraces that we are mortal and imperfect, and in this way, provides a sense of unity among the human race. "Empathy is the invisible hand. It is what allows us to stretch our sensibility with another."

Jeremy Adams Smith wrote, "The old view that we are essentially self-interested creatures is being nudged firmly to one side by evidence that we are also homo empathicus, wired for empathy, social cooperation, and mutual aid" (Krznaric, 2012). Homo-empathic is referring to the idea that we are all naturally empathetic to others. Rifkin argues that "if we are truly homo-empathic, we need to bring out that core nature. If it's repressed by our parenting, our education system, business practices, and our government, our secondary drives come in. The narcissism, the materialism, the violence, the aggression. We need to bring out empathic sociability to prepare the groundwork for an empathic civilization."

THREE MAIN TYPES OF EMPATHY

To utilize empathy, we need to know the three main types of empathy.

- The first is cognitive empathy. This form of empathy is the most accessible and easy to grasp form of empathy. In its most simple form, it is taking the perspective of another person.

- The second is emotional empathy. It is the act of physically feeling an emotion of another person as if it could spread through the air.

- The third is compassionate empathy. It is the same as emotional empathy, but it compels us to take action on these emotions rather than simply feel them.

As marketers, it is our duty to put the customer first. By bringing empathy into our work, we are doing more than just boosting sales. We are able to inspire people to embrace humanity, other perspectives, and tell the stories that need to be told. We have an opportunity to have a strong impact on the world.

Understanding decision-making and empathy is the first step to making this happen. To truly be empathic in our marketing, we need to know to whom we are talking. We need to know what their fears are, what their vices are, what they feel under pressure, what makes them feel empowered, and more.

Read on if you are ready to build trust with your audience and make the world a better place at the same time.

Remember Rifkin's advice: "empathy's goal is solidarity."

THE EMPATHY EQUATION

Now that you know what empathy is, you need to know how to act on it. Throughout this book I will be concluding each chapter with an empathy equation that will simplify two main aspects of empathy that is related to that specific phase of the buyer's journey.

The equation is:

Empathy = Decision-Making + Human Emotion

So how do we apply this equation? We ensure that we make the decision-making process as easy as possible and focus on emotion at every stage of the buyer's journey. In the next five chapters, I will summarize each step of the buyer's journey, how to apply the empathy equation to each, and how to tactfully implement empathy into your marketing strategy.

Below, I explain what each aspect of the empathy equation means and how you can start to wrap your head around them at a high level with tools like the PASE decision framework and emotional intelligence.

UNDERSTANDING DECISION-MAKING

"'Decision' implies the end of deliberation and the beginning of action."—William Starbuck, professor in residence at the University of Oregon's Charles H. Lundquist College of Business (Buchanan and O'Connell, 2006)

As marketers, it is our duty to put the customer first. By bringing empathy into our work, we are doing more than just boosting sales. We are able to inspire people to embrace humanity, other perspectives, and tell the stories that need to be told. We have an opportunity to have a strong impact on the world.

But, how do we make decisions? What takes us from deliberation to action?

As marketers we need to understand two different aspects of decision-making: first, the buyer's journey or the phases that occur prior and after the purchase decision is made; second, the different types of decision-makers using the PASE model (Practical, Action, Social, and Emotional) (Harris, 2020).

Later on, we will go in depth about each of the phases of the buyer's journey and how you can use empathy in an actionable way to build trust with your future buyers.

The phases of the buyer's journey are as follows:

- Need recognition: the buyer acknowledges they have a need for a certain product.

- Informative search: the buyer researches different brands that produce a certain product.

- Alternatives evaluation: the buyer weighs the pros and cons of each brand that produces a certain product.

- Purchase decision: the buyer selects a brand that produces a certain product and purchases it from them.

- Post-purchase: the buyer reflects on the purchase of the product and brand experience and takes action based on their experience.

The PASE decision model argues that there are four different types of decision-makers and that your work should cater to each of them.

The PASE decision-maker's qualities are as follows:

- Practical: responds to logic, can't be pressured, makes rational decisions

The equation is:

Empathy = Decision-Making + Human Emotion

- Action: responds to scarcity, time running out, makes quick decisions

- Social: responds to social proof, follows what others are doing, doesn't want to be left out

- Emotional: responds to photos of people, places, good causes

This is amazing information on human decision-making, but how can marketers take it to the next level? By understanding human em otion on a macro level with the Enneagram. The Enneagram combines human emotion with strategy.

UNDERSTANDING HUMAN EMOTION

According to Chloe Ellis from The Drum, "Emotions have huge action potential and can enable consumers to receive messages they wouldn't accurately perceive in another way, so if brands want to cut through the noise and optimize messaging to drive action, they need to give much more consideration to the power of emotion" (Ellis, 2019). Great marketing takes into account people's thoughts and emotions and how those turn into action.

Throughout this book I will be highlighting stories of marketers who have integrated human emotions into their marketing strategies as well as how they did it and how you and your team can too.

By understanding how people make decisions and how they feel about those decisions, we can create much more meaningful customer experiences. Companies that create experiences rooted in empathy, authenticity, and curiosity are the companies that thrive.

By understanding how people make decisions and how they feel about those decisions, we can create much more meaningful customer experiences. Companies that create experiences rooted in empathy, authenticity, and curiosity are the companies that thrive.

CHAPTER-2

WE ARE ALL NEEDY. COMFORT YOUR CUSTOMERS.

———

Empathy is feeling with people.

—BRENé BROWN

Liquid gold.

When you read those two words, what is the first thing that comes to mind? For most, the answer is the famous processed cheese brand Velveeta.

Whenever someone has the realization that they need a product, that moment on the buyer's journey is called their "need recognition." At this step it is vital to be top of mind for consumers. Velveeta cheese has done this. But what made this cheese so famous? How did it infiltrate American households? How did it become "a staple of the twentieth-century American diet," according to Myles Karp of Vice News?

The first factor is that Velveeta cheese was incredibly easy to manufacture, distribute, and preserve in mass quantities. Second, the brand has personality. Whether the marketing team at Velveeta planned it or not, a well-known sketch comedy show from the 1990s, *In Living Color*, brought humor to the otherwise simple product.

According to Karp, "Any type of cheese can be problematic for the digestive systems of millions of Americans... 75 percent of African Americans, 51 percent of Latinos, and 80 percent of Asian Americans are lactose intolerant, versus the 21 percent of Caucasians. And because minorities historically have been heavily represented in welfare programs, the government wasn't really doing Americans' butts a favor."

In the television show *In Living Color,* a skit capitalized on the humorous yet serious issue of Velveeta/processed cheese and dairy, in general, being a featured food item in most welfare programs.

Archie: Edith! What's for dinner?

Edith: Oh, Archie, it's your favorite! Macaroni and the government cheese!

Archie: Aw, geez, Edith! You know what the government cheese does to me! I spend more time on the throne than Queen Latifah!

I suffer from lactose intolerance and feel very similarly to Archie. While we neither digest the processed cheese, we are still lured in to eat the liquid gold. Why?

A. It is tasty, melty, salty, fatty, etc.—all things humans love to eat. According to the Cleveland Health Clinic, "Some sweet and salty foods and drinks are incredibly addictive. That's why many processed foods are loaded with them" (Cleveland Clinic).

B. Humans are hardwired to want what they can't have, especially if they are raised with it.

Velveeta cheese has a prominent place in my memory, as it was the last resort for my parents to get something into my fussy belly as a child. When I was very young, I would not eat anything but Purdue chicken nuggets, Ellio's Pizza, and Velveeta mac and cheese. I was the biggest fuss-bucket and was basically impossible to feed. My parents wanted me to learn to try new things and refused to make me one of the three very processed options above until I at least tried the other food. As I sat at the dinner table, I silently protested anything healthy and patiently waited for anything that was, well, unhealthy.

I wasn't going to stand for that, so I came up with a plan. I convinced my dad to teach my older brother and me how to make homemade Velveeta Mac and Cheese (the first recipe I memorized) so he and my mom could relax while we made dinner. He taught us, and my brother and I were extremely excited. The next time we were presented with a nasty piece of pork chop or the dreaded broccoli, we had a backup and we didn't need anyone's help to make it. My brother and I were so proud of this incredible accomplishment and even made it for our cousins when they too silently protested for the good stuff. We brought the fun—and the processed foods—to the dinner table.

While our taste buds have significantly evolved, we still pride ourselves in providing liquid gold whenever necessary. It lives on as a staple for our family get-togethers for my four nieces and never fails to bring back memories of pure childhood joy at the dinner table.

EMOTION IN NEED RECOGNITION

This memory is one of millions that people in the country have about Velveeta. Today, the brand understands its place as a nostalgic, relatively unhealthy, processed cheese, and as a result they don't take themselves too seriously. In fact, their social media manager, John Sabine, was an improv comedy actor at Second City Chicago for ten years. This is clear in their social strategy, for example, when Sabine of Velveeta gave the sass back to a Microsoft developer, and it went viral.

The tweet said:

"@crpietschmann:

American #cheese, Cheese Whizm, and #Velveeta @EatLiquidGold are the worst 'cheese' products"

Velveeta replied:

"@EatLiquidGold:

NOT COOL CHRIS - WE DIDN'T SAY ANYTHING WHEN VISTA CAME OUT"

Liquid gold hit the nail on the head with comedy gold and a sprinkle of sass.

I have always had a strong interest in improv comedy. It is stunningly hilarious and rarely disappoints an audience. There are two main reasons why: audience engagement and lack of conflict.

If you are constantly brought into the narrative of what you are watching on stage, as an audience member the experience is a lot more memorable, interactive, and positive. In improv comedy, conflict is the worst case-scenario. The actors focus heavily on affirming the other actors' parts of the story that they are creating live.

This sure sounds a lot like empathy, so, of course, I had to dive into this and learn more.

I reached out to Sabine right away. Sabine has over ten years of experience as a professional improv actor at Second City in Chicago (a source for many of my favorite modern comics like Rachel Dratch, Tina Fey, Amy Poehler, and more). This clearly shows in the way he approaches the social media messaging. Sabine argues that empathy is one of the most important aspects of improv comedy, and he has not stopped using empathy in his daily professional life since taking on his new role of social media manager of liquid gold.

When I interviewed Sabine in December of 2020, he mentioned to me that while running a social media account, it "feels like doing improv comedy. Over ten years in the job has prepared me to support customers in whatever they need right in that moment. My first reaction is to support them. I can read them really quick and execute. There's nothing to plan because you can't plan for the internet. That's so cool." Between constantly changing trends, customer support questions, and more, a social media manager is an improv pro without even knowing it.

A great way to keep up with this constantly changing channel is to utilize empathy, and Sabine mentions that he has his own version of the traditional improv saying, "yes and...." To be truly empathetic and feel what your audience has to say, the phrase has to be "yes, 100 percent." Sabine goes into this concept more by saying, we are often "taught that conflict is what makes a great movie or story. For improv it is the exact opposite. We need no conflict. If someone says, 'man, I hate these books,' you hate them too. It's that simple. Your job is to be a blank slate and to be able to reflect whatever someone's saying, and then to jump 100 percent on board."

According to the publication *The Content Strategist*, improv and marketing is not a new concept. Todd Bieber, former creative director of Upright Citizens Brigade Comedy, has directed over two hundred funny videos for some of the world's biggest brands. In an Advertising Week panel titled "How to Be Funny and Filthy Rich by Making Online Branded Videos," Bieber told marketers that brand videos must prioritize creative content to be successful, rather than featuring a company or product.

What you are about to read is the most simple yet accurate explanation of empathy. By meeting your audience right where they are and agreeing with them 100 percent, you are showing a strong sense of empathy and, in turn, building trust. Sabine mentions, "You're going right to that star with him, and you're saying, 'I'm with you.' No matter what it is, you have to be empathetic. You have to lead with empathy because you have to be able to pick up what they're feeling. And then identify what they're feeling and feel the exact same way back to them." The process of "yes, 100 percent" starts by acknowledging their feelings and meeting them on that "star." The next step is to mirror their feeling back at them. This proves to your audience that you heard exactly what they said to you. Next, understand

When you think in that mindset, you are still making the story and the feeling about you. You are imagining what you would feel if you were in that situation not what your audience is actually feeling. Empathy is feeling exactly what your audience is feeling and feeling it too from their perspective.

how they feel, feel it, and convey that feeling back to them. Let them know you are in the feeling space with them 100 percent.

Improv isn't only a useful skill in marketing but across industries. In a recent study featured in *Academic Medicine*, the authors argued that "health professionals need to learn how to relate to one another to ensure high-quality patient care and to create collaborative and supportive teams in the clinical environment" (Academic Medicine). To train these health professionals, they spent time "teaching empathy during [a] professional training to foster connection and commonality across differences. The authors describe a pilot improvisational theater course and present the preliminary outcomes showing its impact on interprofessional empathy."

You might say, "Pat, this sounds like putting yourself in someone's shoes. We've heard of that. This isn't new."

This is completely different than putting yourself in your audience's shoes.

When you think in that mindset, you are still making the story and the feeling about you. You are imagining what *you* would feel if you were in that situation *not* what your audience is actually feeling. Empathy is feeling *exactly* what your audience is feeling and feeling it too from their perspective.

It is especially critical for brands, because they are not people, to bring humanity to their brand voice. Sabine mentions that as a brand like Velveeta on social media, "You are crashing the human party. Social media is a human party that you are not invited to. So you better do your best human impression and be a human because you can't hide behind your lack of humanity. There's something unsavory about that." The best way to bring humanity to your brand is to show that your brand feels the human emotions that your audience is feeling right now.

As a social media manager, Sabine says, "Empathy and self-awareness have to be at the forefront in whatever you're trying to do. Empathy and humanity have to be the North Star because they can get lost. On the internet at any moment someone's mad, someone's thrilled, someone is anxious. You're getting all the emotions thrown at you at once, and I think the only way to even process that valuably is to say, 'Absolutely. I hear you.'"

From cheese to humans, we can all learn something from meeting people where they are and saying "yes, 100 percent." There will always be value in hearing, acknowledging, and acting on someone else's feelings. By doing so, you bring humanity into your brand. You make your brand stand out. You make your brand more real to people.

Think about when you see a Progressive commercial. Progressive made a great move and put a face to their brand, Flo. In every ad we see from Progressive, Flo is entertaining us in the most relatable, human, and humorous way. Would you really pay attention if the main character wasn't Flo? Since the brand created an identity that speaks to your emotions, you developed a connection (whether you like it or not) and cannot look away. Flo's adventures are short, sweet, hilarious, and, most importantly, human. The writers of Progressive's ads take something we all know—something extremely authentic—and blast it to wild proportions to get our attention and to make us feel something. When a brand makes us feel something, it sticks in our brain and it is very hard to make it leave. When the time comes to choose your new insurance will you go with the relatable Flo or the animated gecko from GEICO, Martin?

DECISION-MAKING IN NEED RECOGNITION

In the empathy equation, we know that understanding the emotions of our audience is only half the story. The other half? Decision-making.

In the need recognition phase, decision-making is not the act of deciding what company to purchase from; rather it is the phase where consumers decide whether or not to even consider a brand. How can you measure these consideration phases? This got me thinking, empathy is important, yes, but I wanted to know how to use it.

What do I mean by that? According to University of California, Berkeley, "Contemporary researchers often differentiate between two types of empathy: 'Affective empathy' refers to the sensations and feelings we get in response to others' emotions; this can include mirroring what that person is feeling, or just feeling stressed when we detect another's fear or anxiety. 'Cognitive empathy,' sometimes called 'perspective taking,' refers to our ability to identify and understand other people's emotions."

Most people are great at cognitive empathy, some are great at affective empathy, but none of us know how to apply empathy better than Daniel Pink. Empathy is a great superpower, but a superpower doesn't do much good until you know how to use it. I turned to one of my favorite learning platforms, MasterClass. MasterClass is the streaming platform that makes it possible for anyone to watch or listen to hundreds of video lessons taught by more than a hundred of the world's best.

Whether it be in business and leadership, photography, cooking, writing, acting, music, or sports, MasterClass delivers a world-class online learning experience. After watching Daniel Pink's MasterClass course on influence, I knew he was a perfect person to talk to about using empathy to gain influence.

Throughout his MasterClass, Dan brought up the concept of information asymmetry and its impact on the business-to-consumer relationship. With an engaging sense of tone and friendly demeanor, Pink describes this phenomenon, "Thanks to the internet and social media, information asymmetry has been replaced by information parity. Now, buyers often have as much (or, in some cases, more) knowledge about a product as sellers. Consumers can tap into an endless stream of choices and comparisons. They also have options for talking back, from leaving a product review on Amazon to disclosing salaries on Glassdoor, further breaking down the structure of information asymmetry." Today, the power is no longer in the company's hands but it is in the consumers' hands. This is nothing too shocking or novel, however. It is easy to forget in the day to day.

Just as Pink highlights in the concept of information asymmetry, brand genius Marty Neumeier highlights on his site that "your brand isn't what you say it is. It's what they say it is." How do we make sure they say the right things then?

With trust.

Empathy has four main aspects according to nurse Theresa Wiseman. On *Psychology Today*'s site, Jessica Schrader highlights that one of the four aspects of empathy is perspective taking. This concept is similar to what I mentioned earlier in this chapter of "yes, 100 percent:" hearing your consumer and acknowledging that their emotions are real. The second aspect is staying out of judgment and approaching said feelings in an unbiased way (Schrader, 2014). Then recognizing the emotion is going from perspective taking and analyzing that perspective to understand what emotion is most prevalent. Lastly, communicating is sharing with the subject that you hear them and know what they are feeling.

Daniel Pink highlights perspective taking by saying that "empathy is the complement to perspective taking. By zeroing in on a buyer's emotions, you're increasing the chances of getting them to act as you wish. Bear in mind that persuasion is a dialogue; it's the hunt for common ground." Ultimately by using the four main aspects of empathy, you are searching for that common ground of trust with your audience, future customers, and current customers. To build and to maintain this trust, it is critical to understand that persuasion is indeed a dialogue. If you are simply throwing messages to the void without considering what your audience is saying and incorporating it into your content, you are doing a disservice to your business. If you listen, understand, go a level deeper, and communicate, you will see results. According to the *Harvard Business Review*, "The top ten companies in the Global Empathy Index 2015 increased in value more than twice as much as the bottom ten, and generated 50 percent more earnings (defined by market capitalization). In our work with clients, we have found a correlation as high as 80 percent between departments with higher empathy and those with high performers" (Parmar, 2016).

I asked Dan how marketers can use empathy to find that common ground in one-way promotions to build trust. He offered three main tactics we can take. These three tactics are how you can engage with potential customers across the four PASE decision models—practical, action, social, and emotional.

1. Go for communications where people have opted in.

A good way of knowing what other people think of your communication is knowing that they've requested it. It's also an act of empathy to get their permission before hitting them with messages that might not be wanted. By allowing people to opt in, we are making the interaction a two-way street with our consumers. They can trust, at a simple level, that you won't spam them with content on channels they did not opt into. They are in control.

2. Use second and third person rather than first person.

Don't say "I." Say "you," or better yet, say "we" and "us." Talking about yourself usually doesn't build affinity; putting things in others' terms does. Without your customers, your company would be nothing. Your marketing needs to reflect that and highlight the importance of your customers' emotions, fears, woes, challenges, etc.

3. Test, test, test.

One of the great things about digital marketing is that you can get pretty good feedback very quickly. For instance, in Dan's email newsletter he almost always tests subject lines. That gives him a sense of what appeals to readers—and, more importantly, what doesn't. Often the reason certain subject lines flop is that we haven't thought of them deeply enough from the receiver's perspective.

Circling back to information asymmetry mentioned above, I asked Dan how information asymmetry has affected empathy.

"Interesting question. Information asymmetry demands empathy and perspective taking at a broad level. If I'm a persuader, I have to understand that you can know almost as much as I do—and that should be the starting point for future communications. At a more tactical level, if persuaders lack an information advantage, they have to enlist other skills, and empathy and perspective taking are among the most important."

In other words, your customers are likely smarter than you.

With the abundance of information on the internet, they may have more time to research your company, your competitors, and the marketplace as a whole. Dan argues that empathy for this fact is critical when trying to persuade someone. Plan as though every potential customer knows more than you and take that perspective in your strategic planning across the organization.

Take a look at brands like Lush, a beauty brand that creates natural beauty products (Ritchie). Instead of framing this feature through the lens of quality, they use Empathy Marketing to let you know they use natural ingredients because they have you in mind. They care about your well-being, your skin, and your beauty. By acting in this way, you are fully allowing the customer to have a seat at the table in business decisions, you are aligned with their emotions about your product, and you know what it will take to build trust with them.

FINALIZING THE EMPATHY EQUATION

From this chapter we identified that in the need recognition phase of the buyer's journey, the empathy equation is:

Empathy = Opting In + A Humanized Brand

John Sabine and Daniel Pink both give us great insight into how we can do both tactfully with our brands. Once you put these steps into action for this phase of the buyer's journey, you will have to meet your customer where they are when they are searching for information on your brand.

PUT IT INTO ACTION

TO MEET YOUR CUSTOMERS IN AN EMOTIONAL AND AUTHENTIC WAY DURING THIS PHASE, YOU CAN USE THE FOLLOWING STRATEGIES.

CULTURE FIRST MARKETING

Culture first marketing is the when a brand moves at the speed of culture and engages with extremely relevant trends. This could be making a meme relevant to their brand; joining a new social platform in a unique, authentic, and compelling way; or joining viral conversations at the right time. The key to culture first marketing is timing. If you join a trend too late as a brand, it comes off as annoying.

MARKET RESEARCH

The definition of market research is the action or activity of gathering information about consumers' needs and preferences. To put this into action, start asking your customers, prospective customers, and past customers questions about your brand. This ensures that real customers' voices are taken into account when you perform marketing activities in the future.

CHANNEL SPECIFIC STRATEGY

Each social network has a dress code. In order to fit each dress code and not sound tone-deaf, ensure that you have a social strategy for each channel you plan to be active on. A strategy that works for Twitter will never work for LinkedIn, and a strategy for TikTok would never work for Facebook. Plan accordingly.

EMPLOYEE ADVOCACY

According to LinkedIn, companies who empower employees to share content perform better. When your employees advocate for your brand, not only do they get more engaged, but you build more trust with your community. As more employees share content, their networks begin to notice your brand in a much more authentic and human-centric way.

CHAPTER-3

EVERYBODY WANTS TO SHINE, BUT HOW?

———

We hear it all the time. The internet is noisy, the internet is crowded, the internet has an information overload.

We hear it all the time because, well, it is extremely true.

The world creates over 33 zettabytes of data every year. Yeah, I had no idea what that meant until I did some research and found Statista's summary of this ambiguous data point. "If you were to burn all of the information created last year onto Blu-ray discs, you would need to invest in an astounding 660 billion—each with a standard capacity of 50 gigabytes. Moving into the biological realm, 33 zettabytes is equivalent to the estimated storage space of 33 million human brains. Delving even deeper, and as an equally impressive testament to the power of DNA, you would need 73 grams of our genetic material to create a backup of our global data" (Armstrong, Statista). Holy s***! More than 33 million human brains would be needed to process the world's data… How can we keep up?

LISTEN, LISTEN, LISTEN = DATA DRIVEN

Thank God for Google. Ever since the company was founded on September 4, 1998, in Menlo Park, California, they have been data focused and have kept tabs on our global data. Of course, they did not do it all alone; however, they have been the go-to for us to find information in this insanely treacherous sea of global data. With access to the same amount of information storage as over thirty-three million brains, imagine if you had the knowledge of Google. How would you use it?

I have always been curious about the data that Google really has access to. Turns out, it's a lot. And it's valuable. Santi Pochat, head of Google's Social Lab, uses the search engine's power to understand his audience on a deeper level and act on it.

If people search "anxiety," their content will focus on calming their audience. According to Pochat, in 2020 the search term "anxiety" hit an all-time high in the onset of a global pandemic, racial injustice, civil unrest, an election, and more. In fact, CNN confirms that, "Google searches for anxiety symptoms from mid-March to mid-May were the highest they've been in the history of the search engine, according to researchers at the Qualcomm Institute's Center for Data Driven Health at the University of California, San Diego" (Prior, 2020).

If people search "love," their content will focus on spreading joy, family, and loved ones.

If people search for a certain trending meme, their content will focus on highlighting that.

Unfortunately, most of us social media managers do not have access to the amount of knowledge and intel Pochat and his

When practicing empathy, it is critical that you remain curious, unbiased, and open to other perspectives.

team have. Yet, we do have access to Google Trends. According to Google's data editor, Simon Rogers, "Google Trends data is an unbiased sample of our Google search data. It's anonymized (no one is personally identified), categorized (determining the topic for a search query) and aggregated (grouped together). This allows us to measure interest in a particular topic across search, from around the globe, right down to city-level geography" (Rogers, 2016).

When practicing empathy, it is critical that you remain curious, unbiased, and open to other perspectives. Google Trends allow us to do that and then some with their robust tools. Rogers mentions that Google Trends "can provide a powerful lens into what Google users are curious about and how people around the world react to important events." However, he argues that you must put the numbers in context. How do you put the numbers in context? "Understanding the percent increase in a search topic can be a useful way to understand how much rise in interest there is in a topic. This percent increase is based on a topic's growth in search interest over a distinct period of time compared to the previous period. Those 'spikes' are a sudden acceleration of search interest in a topic, compared to usual search volume. We know these are interesting because they are often reflective of what's going on in the real world" (Rogers, 2016).

Our work as Empathy Marketers comes from the community management we work on daily. We are at the frontlines of our customers' conversations. We hear their thoughts on our brand. What they love, what they hate, what they wish would improve, and their thoughts. Using this knowledge of our specific audience, we have to also understand what people are feeling around the country and around the world.

We have to understand how our brands, products, and services fit in the context of the lives of the people we sell to, how it fits into the lives of our customers and the lives of our prospects, and more importantly, how can it make their lives better.

If we zoom out to a macro level with Google Trends, we understand more about what content people need in that time. To truly become human-to-human marketers, we need to market with context and compassion.

Pochat mentioned, "As social media professionals, we play an active role in people's lives. We interpret and relay information on a daily basis." It is our job to understand the emotions of our audience and provide value relevant to them in that moment. A social post can have a big impact on someone's association with your brand, depending on their emotion and the copy you write. If you are on their timeline, you are playing an active role in their day. They will remember how you made them feel.

Not only do we listen, we report back to our teams about our audience's behavior. If a post performs well, why? If a post drove a ton of website traffic, why? If a post got more registrants for your upcoming event, why?

We not only reached people's interest, emotion, and heart, but we reached how they think and make decisions.

GET OUT OF YOUR MIND AND INTO THEIRS.

We have to understand how our brands, products, and services fit in the context of the lives of the people we sell to, how it fits into the lives of our customers and the lives of our prospects, and more importantly, how can it make their lives better.

No one understands their audience more than Trndsttrs CEO, Jake Bjorseth. Bjorseth started Trndsttrs to provide large companies glimpses into what matters most to Gen Z so marketers at these brands can gain that deep understanding. Empathy can be used to access Gen Z because they are socially and brand-conscious. A marketer needs to understand what they think, how they feel, and what they think about how they feel.

Why?

Gen Z has a total buying power of over forty-four billion dollars according to IBM in a *Forbes* article, and that number is only going to increase (IBM, 2017). According to Khoros's blog, "Generation Z are the youngest consumers but do not be mistaken, they are not a demographic to ignore....by 2020 [they] are expected to control 40 percent of all consumer shopping. Gen Z is described as anyone born after 1998, which means the generation's oldest members can be found studying at colleges and universities or entering the workforce. According to 93 percent of parents, Gen Z children and young adults are influencing the needs and purchases in households across the country" (Ebel, 2019).

So where do we reach them? They spend over four hours of their day on their mobile devices, on apps, social, and mobile experiences. Brands that do, will not only impress Gen Z but build trust with the audience. When creating experiences for Gen Z, you need to be mobile-first and shareable.

However, a lot of organizations are led by people in much older generations. According to Korn Ferry, "The average Chief Marketing Officer age is fifty-two, with CMOs in the life sciences and professional services sectors the oldest average age at fifty-four. The youngest average age of CMOs is fifty in the consumer sector" (Korn Ferry, 2017). As a result, marketing leaders may have a bit of a language barrier to Gen Z. So, how can Fortune 500 companies, startups, and small businesses connect with Gen Z in a meaningful way?

Get to know them. Have an advocate for them. Interact with them.

Like many people did in 2020 and beyond, I became obsessed with TikTok. This Gen Z- and Millennial-focused platform has one simple mission—to inspire creativity and bring joy (TikTok, 2021). The platform embraces this mission by making it incredibly easy to enjoy with full-screen videos, simple user experience design, and incredible in-app creation tools for their pool of over one billion active users.

I started using the platform to bring myself joy in a dark time. I found myself dancing, lip syncing to my favorite songs, acting out some of my favorite scenes, and more. Let's be clear. I am not a dancer, lip sync pro, or an actor, but I had fun, got pretty good reach, and I was getting to know an audience I would not normally reach with Twitter and LinkedIn.

Why is TikTok winning? It's designed with a mobile-first mindset.

According to Zebra IQ's 2020 State of Gen Z Report, there are three billion people in Gen Z worldwide (35 percent of the global population), and they are a mobile-first generation. While that information is critical in understanding them, the best way to connect and build trust with Gen Z is through empathy. Once they know that their perspective is heard, they will trust you a lot more (ZebraIQ, 2020).

Jake Bjorseth, the Founder and CEO of Trndsttrs, started his agency to help companies do just that. Bjorseth's mission is to advocate for Gen Z and ensure that their point of view is not only respected but integrated into his clients' strategies. He shares why empathy means so much by saying, "Empathy is probably the number one characteristic for any individual working in marketing because if you can't understand the problems and pains that people face, then your marketing is never going to get anywhere. The best marketing at the end of the day needs to solve some sort of a problem. It's not about the glitz and the glamour and the cool video. It's really about a deep understanding of your audience because once you have that understanding, you can develop insights that others just wouldn't be able to do." Even Social Media Today agrees by stating, "Honesty, empathy, and social consciousness will win on social" (Wiltshire, 2020).

Jake and his team specialize in creating communities of like-minded individuals on platforms like Discord, Slack, and more. They use these spaces to get genuine insights into what Trndsttrs' clients want to know. He mentions that they don't just focus on private platforms but also social media. "We're always doing both quantitative and qualitative research," he says, "because I love quantitative on a larger demographic perspective, but from a psychographic I prefer qualitative research. We'll do focus groups, beta groups, test apps, test websites, test marketing material before it goes out to the audience. Then on the quantitative side, we do a lot of surveys with variations so it is customized for the consumer. We'll send something out with the goal of not receiving the exact same thing. Then based on their answers, we find common themes."

Trndsttrs does a lot of interesting things to gather the data, but the next part is most important.

"We analyze that data by computing it and working internally with our team to form hypotheses. These insights could potentially lead a focus group as well to then turn those insights into strategies and into what we should do about it." Empathy is about being curious about how your audience is feeling right now, understanding it with them, describing those feelings, and acting on those feelings. Jake and his team hit on all four of these with his process.

He also understands that empathy is a two-way street. "Tapping into the Gen Z sphere is difficult, and I certainly have empathy for older marketers when trying to understand this very elusive generation because it constantly changes over time. These platforms they're on and the video styles and ad styles you have to make to get their attention are difficult."

Everything is in a constant state of change, and that is hard. However, if you don't keep up you will be left behind, not trusted, and see a lot less revenue. NPR highlighted some research that the American Psychological Association conducted, and they "found that teens report feeling even more stressed than adults, and that this affects them in unhealthy ways. Approximately 30 percent of the 1,018 teens surveyed reported feeling sad, overwhelmed or depressed, and 25 percent said they had skipped meals because of their anxiety" (Fraga, 2017). If brands neglect to acknowledge the real issues each generation faces, they will not build trust with the audiences they want. Worse, they will come off tone-deaf.

In Zebra IQ's report, they share how Gen Z thinks about communication, fashion, trends, money, work, activism, and more. They share how marketers can talk the talk of Gen Z by:

1. Thinking mobile-first;

2. Understanding trending emojis and memes;

3. Looking into all possible interpretations of your creatives; and

4. Leaning into it if you are trending.

They mention that "being first to trends authentically can help you win over Gen Z's wallet."

Gen Z is always looking for the next thing, and they are always looking for sources of authenticity. According to some research that CNBC conducted on Gen Z, "Gen Z craves a personal, authentic connection. We grew up watching and interacting with YouTube stars who were just like us, not elusive, Hollywood celebrities. As such, we appreciate the chance to engage with authentic, imperfect art," is one way of summing up how this generation feels (Handley, 2018).

This stems from their value-driven mentality: "Gen Z is very perceptive of the brands they buy from and the places they want to work at. Their strong values are human rights, environmental aid, political reform, and education for all." Understanding that Gen Z is in need of being heard, authenticity and value alignment are the first steps that any brand should take. These attributes make social media and community more important than ever. For example, take a look at the top three most-loved Gen Z brands according to a Morning Consult report: Google, Netflix, and YouTube. Now, let's zoom into each of their missions (Morning Consult, 2019).

Google: to organize the world's information and make it universally accessible and useful (Google).

Netflix: to entertain the world (Netflix).

YouTube: to give everyone a voice and show them the world (YouTube).

The striking similarity? The word "world." Each brand believes, understands, and embraces that their brand is for everyone. Gen Z is the most socially conscious generation and it is not surprising that the missions of their top three brands align with the generation's mission. Understanding that we are all equal, all deserving, and all one is empathy at its core. Brands that will win will take note of this.

How can you build communities for your brand? With empathy. Jake highlights that "it's about understanding your audience's emotions and how their brain ultimately got them to those emotions. It isn't about finding the problem and solving it. It is about understanding the steps people go through in identifying that problem. At least you can understand what that step-by-step process looks like. It is that deeper level of understanding of the rationale to get there." It is not just about feeling what your audience is feeling but also about thinking what they are thinking. Jake argues that this can't be too hard because today "people tend to either wear their emotions on their sleeve (on social media) or you can kind of dig it out when talking with them."

EMPATHY = EMOTIONAL DATA + AUTHENTICITY/ADVO- CATING FOR YOUR AUDIENCE

As a marketing professional, it is your job to listen, interpret, communicate, and advocate for your audience. This is taking the concept of inviting your customer to every meeting to the next level. If your company does not have someone constantly thinking about the voice of the customer, it is time to do that. To fully embody empathy in your brand, you need to understand what emotions your audience are feeling based on what they are searching, and you need to acknowledge the different barriers across generations and speak to them with authenticity while advocating for your audience. Empathy is a trend that everyone can get behind, not just Gen Z.

PUT IT INTO ACTION

TO MEET YOUR CUSTOMERS IN AN EMOTIONAL AND AUTHENTIC WAY DURING THIS PHASE, YOU CAN USE THE FOLLOWING STRATEGIES.

SEO

"Without empathy, my clients would miss out on thousands of site visits per month. My clients are therapists, so their ideal keywords often overlap with those of the medical industry. My clients simply can't compete with sites like WebMD and Healthline, so we have to creatively research keywords using empathy.

By stepping into the minds of my clients, I can find longtail keywords that target more obscure symptoms or behaviors. Instead of targeting "anxiety," we target "why can't I fall asleep at night?" Instead of "depression," we target "can't stop feeling bad about myself." The opportunities are endless!

—KRISTIE PLANTINGA, FOUNDER OF THERAPIE SEO

ETHNOGRAPHY AND NETNOGRAPHY

Ethnography is by definition the scientific description of the customs of individual peoples and cultures, and netnography is the same, just on the internet. To gather this information, you metaphorically have to go into the subject's shoes and understand what their day-to-day life is like. By doing this, you build a strong sense of empathy for a person or set of people, and you can take action on those insights in your marketing strategy.

FOCUS GROUPS

Focus groups are a research tactic where you have a conversation with a group of people you are trying to learn more about. This research, if done right and equitably, allows marketing practitioners to take an extremely human-centric approach to their strategy moving forward.

SURVEYS

We've all seen surveys that aren't very impressive. The key is to construct surveys that ask questions about problems your customers face. To ensure these surveys are truly authentic and empathetic, keep some questions open ended and read every response.

CHAPTER-4

YOU AREN'T THE ONLY OPTION: STOP ACTING LIKE IT.

Let's set a scene.

You are getting ready to visit your family out of state and you have a layover on the way. Your first flight goes shockingly well—no excessive noise, no one drooling on your shoulder, and you were able to get a good amount of work done. On the next flight, you are going to reward yourself with a nice movie.

As you are landing at the layover destination, there is an announcement on the intercom, "For those boarding the layover from this flight, we are sorry to say that the flight has been canceled."

Damnit, you think, *I am sure they will help us find a new flight or at least give us somewhere to stay for the night.* So, you remain calm but are a little bummed out.

As you get off the plane, you are greeted with a line of furious passengers waiting at the help desk. The intercom shocks everyone and mentions, "There will be no vouchers for the next flight that was canceled. Please come back tomorrow to board the replacement flight to your destination. Thank you for flying." You can't believe what you are hearing, and you go to the closest airport bar you can find to get a drink and a nice meal. As you enjoy your airport dining, you realize your cousin Laura lives about twenty minutes away. You call her, and she is delightfully surprised and is happy to have you stay the night.

On your way over to Laura's house, however, you make it clear with that airline (like many others have) that this was unacceptable. Not so many people are lucky to have a cousin Laura in every city they have a layover in. You share your story in a tweet, and it gets a lot of traction, responses, and empathy but none of that comes from the airline. Unfortunately for the airline, your following on Twitter is massive, and you are shocked you heard nothing from the airline. You decide you won't be flying with them tomorrow as you are greeted by cousin Laura.

Now, how does that make you feel?

This is a true story.

LISTEN, LISTEN, LISTEN

An airline forgot to listen to their customers on social media and respond in an empathetic way. This caused a tweet about that airline to gain a lot of attention and, in turn, a lot less business for the airline.

Now, this didn't happen to her, but Christina Garnett, a member of the community team at HubSpot, shared this story with me to help us understand the role social listening plays in empathy. The first step? Curiosity.

To truly embrace empathy for your audience you need to be curious about them, who they are, what they need, and what they feel. Curiosity killed the cat, but lack of curiosity kills the marketer. Garnett is largely known for her empathy on social media as a personal brand, and she attributes that to her innate curiosity for people and her network. She has built the community of Marketing Twitter through empathy toward other marketers. Garnett ties her community-building skills to curiosity and mentions that "if you aren't curious, you're not going to care. That's really the root of it. You have to want to know more and want to learn more from people. I've never met a curious person who thought they knew it all. They're curious because they know there's so much more they can understand, and they know that process is never over, just like empathy. Being truly empathetic is never over."

Curiosity is the understanding that you will always have something to learn. This is extremely similar to empathy (you always can learn something from empathy) and similar to the Enneagram (you can always learn something from the Enneagram). Learning is a lifelong commitment, not a one-and-done job.

While Garnett is curious in her personal life, she also shares how this has helped her in her professional life. "For me, I find that my curiosity works in tandem with empathy. I do a lot with social listening. Even when I'm on Twitter, I actively am listening to determine sentiment mood. Honestly, as an empath, I can read emotions in a room, whether that room is online, written, or physical. So I find there's opportunity

To truly embrace empathy for your audience you need to be curious about them, who they are, what they need, and what they feel. Curiosity killed the cat, but lack of curiosity kills the marketer.

there for marketers and that curiosity helps us because curiosity feeds empathy." Reading the room is a skill we all need to have as people but even more so as marketers. Today, the line between tone-deaf and groundbreaking content is really blurred. There have been countless examples of tone-deaf marketing campaigns that are not empathetic to the current events, what their audience needs in that time, and how their audience feels about the content they shared. Without thinking about empathy, a brand could commit suicide with just one tone-deaf post and lose a lot in sales.

Christina recalls the airline story from before and mentions that when the airline "didn't do anything, didn't do a single thing," they left a lasting impression on that person's gut feeling about the brand. They also left a strong impression on her followers (thousands of people) and beyond.

So how can we as marketers ensure we embrace empathy and listen to our customers?

SOCIAL LISTENING

Christina shares that social listening and social monitoring are not the same. "Social monitoring is a short game. You want to respond and resolve quickly. Social listening is a long game. You want to use this information to impact the brand positively over time—determine ways to improve, cultivate relationships with your audience, and gain customers over your competitors." Social monitoring is seeing conversations, quickly resolving them, and moving on. Social listening is seeing those conversations, interpreting what the deeper level of that tweet is, understanding how those people are feeling, feeling it with them, and incorporating that into content strategy.

"That's really the root of it. You have to want to know more and want to learn more from people. I've never met a curious person who thought that they knew it all. They're curious because they know that there's so much more that they can understand, and they know that that process is never over, just like empathy. Being truly empathetic is never over."

Christina offers concrete things to look for. "Do you see trends? What do customers love? Hate? Is there an opportunity to connect with your audience? Are there commonalities where you can showcase that you care and can take action to ensure the negative experiences happen less often? Are there opportunities to create super fans out of your regular customers?"

Listen to your audience. Be curious. Empathy will come.

Like Epictetus, a Greek Stoic philosopher, famously said, "We have two ears and one mouth so that we can listen twice as much as we speak."

Epictetus would have made a fabulous marketer.

As we work in our day-to-day routines, we marketers can get caught up in what our focus is. When this happens, we stop listening. We start writing content and putting it out to the rest of the world without listening. That doesn't seem to empathetic to me.

So, as marketers, how do we ensure we listen? How can we use social listening effectively? Here's how.

In Socialbakers's report "Social Media Listening: An Essential Marketing Tool," the difference between the two are as follows: "Social monitoring is simply the process of collating, identifying, and responding to these brand mentions. For example, a large brand might employ members of its social media team to watch for @ mentions on Twitter and respond to them in a timely manner. Social listening is more complex and refers to using the data from these individual interactions to draw broader conclusions. Social listening can give

Listen to your audience. Be curious. Empathy will come.

you an extraordinary amount of critical insight into customer sentiment, industry trends, and brand awareness" (Li, 2021).

The main differentiator is that you are using what is "heard" on social media and making a conclusion about it. Understanding the existing conversations about your brand and your industry will help you write with empathy that is relevant to your audience right now. According to Sprout Social, you can use five main strategies to make conclusions about your audience and take action. See the end of this chapter for the full explanation of each (Sprout Social, 2021).

In the Socialbakers report they found that "only 8 percent of brands who leveraged a listening solution utilized it for competitive research and analysis." Only 8 percent… If you could understand the conversations about your competitors in real time, why wouldn't you? That is a power we have that many marketers could never dream of in the past. Use the information you find in the conversations about your competition to frame your product as 1) better, and 2) more trustworthy.

Li argues that "the question going forward is not whether or not brands will need to adopt a listening solution—social listening will undoubtedly become an indispensable marketing function for most consumer-facing brands, especially as listening technology continues to improve." I'd argue the same about empathy.

In marketing, trends are not a question of if but when. It is only a matter of time that companies all over the world realize the power of focusing on empathy and make it an integral part of their social listening strategy. According to the Global Marketing Alliance, "Empathic listening means listening with the intent to understand, to get inside another person's frame of reference or world view. When you truly understand your audience, you can focus on problem-solving—showing how you can help your audience overcome their challenges and achieve their goals with your product or service" (Wise, 2017). Simply put, the only way you can solve your customers' problems is by fully understanding who your customers are.

ENSURE YOUR BRAND STORY IS, WELL, A TRUE STORY

When marketers develop brands, they focus on developing a brand story. According to HubSpot, "A brand story recounts the series of events that sparked your company's inception and expresses how that narrative still drives your mission today. Just like your favorite books and movies' characters, if you can craft a compelling brand story, your audience will remember who you are, develop empathy for you, and, ultimately, care about you" (Chi, 2020).

Essentially a brand story makes your brand memorable, relatable, and authentic. The key word? Authentic. "Whether you're publishing your brand story on your website or using it to inform your overall mission, make sure it's fact, not fiction. Spitting out a highlight reel, like almost every other brand does, won't actually resonate with people. Instead, it's crucial you tell the honest truth about the adversity your company has faced and how you're working to overcome it. Because what people relate to and get inspired by isn't endless success. It's the rocky journey of pursuing a goal, getting knocked down, and, ultimately, finding a path toward success" (Chi, 2020). A lot of negativity can come to a brand if they don't share their full journey with their customers, future customers, and community. Today's consumers expect the truth. They expect honesty. Gone are the days of sweeping the "hard stuff" under the rug. Your brand story is your mission, and your audience expects you to live that mission with full transparency.

What happens when you don't?

Headlines. The bad kind.

In early 2021, a few stock rookies got together on the social platform Reddit to plan a mass purchase of the company GameStop's stock. The company was set to fail due to the digital-first world we live in according to the hedge funds surrounding the company, and the Redditers wanted to play Robinhood and make the hedge funds pay up to GameStop for betting against them. The funniest part? They used the app Robinhood to make these bulk investments. After all, Robinhood's mission/brand story is to "Let the People Trade."

The news was going wild, and Wall Street was full of confusion. To put Wall Street at ease, Robinhood halted all trading on the GameStop stocks. Well, you may know what happens next. Outrage.

According to CNN, "A Robinhood customer filed a class-action lawsuit against the stock-trading app after the company barred traders from buying shares of GameStop promoted by WallStreetBets, a popular Reddit group for investors. The lawsuit, filed in the Southern District of New York, claims that Robinhood's actions rigged the market against its customers.

"Robinhood's actions were done purposefully and knowingly to manipulate the market for the benefit of people and financial institutions who were not Robinhood's customers," the lawsuit states (Alfonso III, 2021).

Not only was Robinhood compromising the financial well-being of their customers, but they were going against their brand story and their mission. Time will tell what happens from this issue, but I think companies that offer similar services and show empathy to their own customers (as well as Robinhood customers) will win. For example, their rival Public whose mission is "to open the stock market to everyone by making it inclusive, educational, and fun," shared the following tweet in the midst of the Robinhood drama: "We're back. Our clearing firm, Apex, has resumed the ability to buy $GME, $AMC, and $KOSS on Public. We appreciate their cooperation and are grateful to our members for their patience and understanding" (@Public, January 28, 2021).

In addition to this support, they also made it clear that customers from other apps could transfer all of their stocks to Public by saying, "We're so excited to see our community massively expanding. The team is working hard through the weekend to approve and transfer accounts. We appreciate your patience and look forward to seeing you in the app soon." They acted quickly, and they acted with empathy. How? They listened to their audience, and they acted according to their brand story/mission with empathy.

EMPATHY = LISTEN + MISSION

If you aren't paying attention to your market, you aren't marketing. Find the conversations that mention your brand, are relevant to your brand, or mention your competitors' brands. As you listen, ensure you are maintaining a proactive mindset based on your brand story/mission. If you don't, well, you know. S*** hits the fan.

PUT IT INTO ACTION

To meet your customers in an emotional and authentic way during their alternative evaluation phase, you can use the following strategies.

REVIEWS

Reviews are a goldmine for marketers and sales people. If you aren't reading G2, TrustPilot, Yelp or whatever your industry gets reviews on, you are missing out on product strategy intel and marketing strategy intel. In addition to looking at your company's own reviews, look at your competitors' reviews. What are the pain points they have using your competitors' products? Solve them.

SOCIAL LISTENING

Social listening, by definition, is the process of monitoring social media channels for mentions of your brand, competitors, product, and more. This process is like having a focus group, market research study, and ethnography all in one. Social listening allows you and your team to understand the themes of conversations around your brand. To practice empathy, use these conversations and talk to them in your promotion.

FIVE STRATEGIES ACCORDING TO SPROUT SOCIAL:

STRATEGY 1: BRAND HEALTH

Understanding the public perception of your brand or your most important products is an essential starting point to taking your strategy to the next level. You'll get insight into the positive or negative feelings people associate with your brand and the specific traits and features that spark their attention.

This can challenge you to rethink assumptions and lead to much more targeted marketing.

STRATEGY 2: INDUSTRY INSIGHTS

Social listening helps you pick up on industry trends before they even become trends. By analyzing hashtags or discussions within your industry, you can get a better sense of where your market is headed. This can help you create or reposition products, content, and general messaging that will become a key talking point as trends develop.

STRATEGY 3: COMPETITIVE ANALYSIS

Social media is a competitive channel for brands, and some of Sprout's most popular social media reports are those that customers use to track their competition.

STRATEGY 4: CAMPAIGN ANALYSIS

Brands spend a good deal of their time coming up with new campaigns to launch, but without insight into whether or not that campaign succeeded, they have no information about how to improve or build upon those efforts.

STRATEGY 5: EVENT MONITORING

While you may already be using a hashtag for your event or conference, you might miss out on mentions of your event by just the title or associated key terms like session titles, speakers, and key themes. Setting up listening queries around your events ensures you get the full picture, including both positive feedback and areas of improvement, and that you maximize the business opportunities of your efforts, like identifying additional potential leads.

AUDIENSE

Audiense is a platform that takes social listening and brings it to a whole other level. Audiense is an advanced audience intelligence solution, which provides detailed insights about any audience to drive your social marketing strategy with actionable and enriched real-time data to deliver genuine business results. The platform highlights *who* your audience is and social listening highlights *what* they are saying.

From a conversation directly with Audiense's CEO:

"Audiense helps marketers improve empathy mainly in two ways:

The first one is by providing audience personality insights, with tons of literature about how to write and what visuals to choose depending on their needs and values. Marketers can inform their tone and creativity based on this information.

The second one would be our segmentation by interconnectivity. Doing this allows you to better understand your communities within your audience and therefore look at the possible different points of views within a topic or affinities for those communities within your audience."

CHAPTER-5

FROM DOUBT
TO DELIGHT

———

Like many other professionals, I am always looking for ways to improve my growth in my career and my abilities. This accelerated with the pandemic starting in 2020 because, well, I had more time. According to Google Trends, so did a lot of other people. The search volume for the phrase "certification" went up from an index score of 40 in March 2020 to an index score of 100 in January 2021. (This means that January 2021 was the most popular time over the past five years.)

To cure my craving to learn, I turned to MasterClass for some solid inspiration. As I was browsing through their list of amazing individuals, I found an incredible course from Chris Voss. If you don't know him already, Voss spent over twenty-four years at the Federal Bureau of Investigation as the lead international kidnapping negotiator. He gained his expertise in negotiation from Harvard Law School, the FBI, and Scotland Yard (The Black Swan Group, 2021). In other words, Voss gets people and emotion. He was trained to.

While marketers do not have as much on the line as Voss did in his career, our goal is to negotiate with our audience why they should trust us and buy our product or service. As I studied his work, I was pumped to see that empathy was an integral part of Voss's strategy. Voss mentions that it is critical that you are "building trust-based influence through the use of tactical empathy or deliberately influencing the other side's feelings. By appealing to your counterpart's emotions, you can build rapport, mutual understanding, influence, and—ultimately—deals" (MasterClass, 2021).

The purchase decision phase of the customer journey can not only be accelerated by empathy, but it can also become a lot more enjoyable for both parties involved. Because this is the second-to-last step in the customer journey and the moment that the customer decides that they trust you and want to buy from you, making it easy for them to trust you with empathy for their situation is key. In this phase of the customer journey, you want it to be memorable, frictionless, and exciting!

Whether you are negotiating with a team of five people at another company for your B2B product or you are selling a direct-to-consumer product and your item is in the customer's cart, this moment is critical for your revenue and brand reputation.

As a social media professional, I get bombarded with new products I could try for the accounts I manage probably three to five times a week. I know, it is a lot. What's worse? When I actually need a new product, the process of buying a software is most often painful. You get a demo, they ask you how you like it, then they email you a case study and hound you until you make your final decision.

As you may be able to tell, this has been my experience first-hand and I don't love it. However, one day a social media tool made my buyer's journey delightful. Yes, delightful. Let me tell you why. They put the power in my hands from the beginning by saying, "There is no pressure to commit to using the product by a certain date. Just let us know how it goes. Is there any way we can support you right now?"

They asked me a question that 1) made me feel heard and supported, and 2) would make me answer in a way that gave them great insight further down the selling process. I was able to inform them that the product was meeting expectations in most areas and missed one feature I was looking for. Later on in my buyer's journey, they addressed that expectation they had failed on, explaining what they were going to do to improve on it, and I was sold.

They used empathy. Perfectly. And you can too. Voss shares two helpful tips on empathy and how you can use it in negotiations of any kind.

"Have a calibrated question—a how or what question calibrated more for emotional impact than for conveying information. The calibrated question can lead to increased empathy for your position and give the other side the illusion of control.

Employ tactical empathy—the deliberate influencing of your negotiating counterpart's emotions for the ultimate purpose of building trust-based influence and securing deals. The ways you employ your voice, labels, mirrors, and dynamic silence all contribute to tactical empathy" (MasterClass, 2021).

The main lesson from these two empathy strategies is that your customer is in control of the purchase decision and empowering them through the buying process is key. This will make them feel empowered, in control, and ultimately more satisfied with their decision to purchase your product or service. Not only does this matter in the purchase decision but throughout the entire customer journey. If your potential customer feels they are not being heard or do not have control, they will stop considering your product or service immediately.

You can empower your customers by doing things that don't scale and by making emotional intelligence a habit and practice for you and your team.

DO THINGS THAT DON'T SCALE

Paul Graham is the cofounder at Y Combinator, the first of a new type of startup incubator. Since 2005, Y Combinator has funded over two thousand startups, including Airbnb, Dropbox, Stripe, and Reddit. In July 2013, Graham posted a famous blog post titled "Do Things That Don't Scale," and it opened with, "One of the most common types of advice we give at Y Combinator is to do things that don't scale. A lot of would-be founders believe that startups either take off or don't. You build something, make it available, and if you've made a better mousetrap, people beat a path to your door as promised.

"Or they don't, in which case the market must not exist. Actually, startups take off because the founders make them take off. There may be a handful that just grew by themselves, but usually it takes some sort of push to get them going. A good metaphor would be the cranks that car engines had before they got electric starters. Once the engine was going, it would

The main lesson from these two empathy strategies is that your customer is in control of the purchase decision and empowering them through the buying process is key. This will make them feel empowered, in control, and ultimately more satisfied with their decision to purchase your product or service. Not only does this matter in the purchase decision but throughout the entire customer journey. If your potential customer feels they are not being heard or do not have control, they will stop considering your product or service immediately.

You can empower your customers by doing things that don't scale and by making emotional intelligence a habit and practice for you and your team.

keep going, but there was a separate and laborious process to get it going" (Graham, 2020). He continues the blog post by sharing multiple ways new companies can do things that don't scale, but the most relevant to our conversation on Empathy Marketing is delight and the experience.

Empathy Marketing helps get people to learn more about your product or service because they feel heard. Next, you want to build trust, and trust comes from an amazing customer experience. Graham refers to delight: "You should take extraordinary measures not just to acquire users, but also to make them happy. For as long as they could (which turned out to be surprisingly long), Wufoo sent each new user a hand-written thank you note. Your first users should feel that signing up with you was one of the best choices they ever made." And for the customer experience, "It's not the product that should be insanely great, but the experience of being your user." When companies delight and create undeniably great experiences, their customers will notice, and more customers will come.

A perfect example of this tactic happened at the end of 2020. A viral video sensation landed on TikTok from a user named Nathan Apodaca, or doggface208 on TikTok. It was a selfie video of Apodaca lip syncing to "Dreams" by Fleetwood Mac on his longboard. Simple, yet impactful. Here is what Apodaca shared with the Drum: "So I grabbed my juice, my board, and I started walking to work. On the highway, you have to go uphill before you go down. So on the way up, I'm walking and looking at my favorites list. I came across 'Dreams' inside my favorite list, and I'm like, 'Okay, this is going to be the song.' I started going downhill. I'd seen that the road curved. I was like, okay, I can skate down that, get the video, and then be good. And then I started going."

Ocean Spray could have seen this video and simply shared it on Twitter or commented on the TikTok, but they decided to do something that would never scale and that would never be forgotten. "It turns out that Apodaca was in fact longboarding to work after his car battery had died, and so over a week after his video went viral, Ocean Spray delivered him a new one, laden with bottles of Cran-Raspberry. Then, inspired by the video, Ocean Spray's chief exec Tom Hayes hopped on his skateboard to record his own version" (Watson, 2020). The simple fact of the matter is that Ocean Spray did not have to do *any* of that. They would continue to earn revenue for their products had they done little to nothing. They made the conscious and deliberate decision to support Apodaca as a customer and as a human. They chose empathy.

MAKE EMOTIONAL INTELLIGENCE (EQ) A HABIT

Empathy is talked about a lot. The word is being used more and more, but do people even know what it means anymore? Do people even know how to act on empathy? Do people still know how to feel other people's emotions and not just theirs?

With the word being used more across industries, curiosity on empathy has seen a dramatic increase. According to Google Trends, the search term "empathy" has gone up in frequency and hit a peak in September 2020.

The top five search queries with empathy in them were "sympathy vs. empathy," "what is empathy," "define empathy," "sympathy and empathy," and "lack empathy." This makes it clear that people are realizing two main things about empathy. First, they don't actually know what it means, and second, they believe that they lack it. I am not the only one finding this trend and doing something about it.

Maya Malekian and Geneve Lau, both students at Boston University, started a collective of students in 2020 by the name of Empath Worldwide with one mission—to create synergy between creatives and organizations to turn aspirations into action. Empath Worldwide was started to offer pro bono public relations services.

Malekian shares why the team created Empath Worldwide. "In the classroom, we kept hearing the word empathy being used. Our professors kept focusing on empathy when it comes to communicating with your stakeholders, whether it's internal or external. It is an important thing to be thinking about, and we heard it so many times we thought there was something meaningful about the word.

"There's a reason why companies who are empathetic are the ones who are able to connect the most with their audiences. When we thought about what we can do as students who were figuring out what our next step was when a pandemic hit, we thought we would create something that would allow us to keep doing the things that we love, and so that's why we started this collective of students who really want to hone their craft."

Empath Worldwide runs their engine of creativity with six main principles spelling out EMPATH: engagement, mobility, passion, adaptability, tenacity, and honesty. It is clear that they embodied empathy from the start as they started their collective because they knew other students who were feeling the same thing.

Malekian shares more about their core values by saying, "Our core values spell out EMPATH because all those core values rely on empathy in order to be successful. In order to practice engagement and mobility and honesty and all those things, you have to be empathetic for those things to actually be successful. You can be honest, but brutal honesty is something that no one really likes because it's not rooted in empathy." This is such a key lesson on setting core values for companies and communicating those values. If they are not rooted in empathy and the principles of empathy, they are not valuable to your organization internally or externally.

Lau also shares a strong point by saying, "When we hear 'empathy' and the phrase 'being an empathetic communicator' thrown around a lot, especially like thought leadership pieces, there is never a step-by-step explanation or magic formula of how to apply empathy. It's really different for every scenario. It starts with having to understand empathy, outside of the professional world, as a human being. Then it's complicated because, how do you take this kind of life skill and this concept and apply it to communications and still keep its essence true? You realize that it's more of a framework and a mindset rather than a recipe and checking boxes."

BOOM!

Lau hit the nail on the head.

Empathy is not about checking boxes; it is a mindset. The best way to use this mindset? A framework. What framework? Malekian and Lau use a framework called design thinking. This is the framework used specifically by the Empath Worldwide team. This is not the only framework teams can use to make empathy a habit but is one solid option.

Lau mentions that "design thinking is an ideation process that was developed at Stanford, a college whose focus is

Lau also shares a strong point by saying, "When we hear 'empathy' and the phrase 'being an empathetic communicator' thrown around a lot, especially like thought leadership pieces, there is never a step-by-step explanation or magic formula of how to apply empathy. It's really different for every scenario. It starts with having to understand empathy, outside of the professional world, as a human being. Then it's complicated because, how do you take this kind of life skill and this concept and apply it to communications and still keep its essence true? You realize that it's more of a framework and a mindset rather than a recipe and checking boxes."

around empathy. The process features five steps: empathize, define, ideate, prototype, and test. Although it is a linear process, some steps, like prototype and test, involve more back and forth." She continues by saying that "the only way to really develop solutions for companies is to understand their audience on a micro level. Gone are the days of hypothetical inferences. Now, there is a dire need to dig deep and understand people holistically and to act accordingly."

Professionals who use design thinking heavily are user experience designers. They often have to put themselves in the end user's position and have empathy for them and how the product will be for them. The Interaction Design Foundation, a learning platform for user experience designers, highlights the five steps of design thinking in the following way:

- Empathize with your audience.

- Define their needs, problems, and the insights you can gather on them.

- Ideate by challenging assumptions and creating ideas for innovative solutions.

- Prototype—start creating solutions.

- Test—execute these solutions.

(Interaction Design Foundation, 2020).

As a communications professional, your role is to take these five steps and incorporate them into your client's strategies. It does not have to be in that exact order, but all five of these elements should be top of mind. By focusing on design thinking and rooting each of these steps with empathy, your stakeholders, both internally and externally, will trust you more and, in turn, buy more.

Lau shares four phases of the design thinking process, and I highlight how we can put empathy into practice in each one:

- Understand and Empathize: In this first step of the design thinking process, it's really important that we fully understand the client and their needs. Most of all, we obviously can have our own opinions on the space the client is inhibiting, but the focus should be on the client and how they paint their perspective without you bringing in your own preexisting ideas.

- Define: This step is about making the scope of work or defining what exactly a partnership with a marketing practitioner and a client entails. By setting the bounds, it makes the vision clearer for what we are trying to achieve.

- Ideate: Here we are able to really utilize the creativity in our industry and throw out as many ideas as we can. Obviously, the client is going to come in with their idea of what outcomes they want to have, but I think it's important that the marketing practitioner also brings some of their own ideas to the table that might spark some new ideas.

- Prototype and Test: It's really important to test things out, get a second eye, or get some feedback before things are really implemented for good. Obviously, with bigger agencies you can run focus groups, but I think the very basis of it—having people from different teams on both the client side and the agency side to look over and give feedback—is just as good.

- Implement: This is simple enough, just the actual implementation of the thing itself.

- Evaluate and Reflect: This, and then repeat.

When going through this process, keep your audience, customer, or client at the center of everything you do. It will help you create unscalable, memorable, and empathetic user experiences that will, in turn, result in more success.

EMPATHY = UNSCALABLE + EMOTIONAL INTELLIGENCE AS A HABIT

At the end of the day, to make your product the final fit, you have to do things that don't scale and that bring emotional intelligence to the forefront of your strategy. Listen to customer feedback, research why your carts are abandoned, and you will learn a lot.

PUT IT INTO ACTION

TO MEET YOUR CUSTOMERS IN AN EMOTIONAL AND AUTHENTIC WAY DURING THIS PHASE, YOU CAN USE THE FOLLOWING STRATEGIES.

CONVERSATIONAL MARKETING

According to Drift, conversational marketing is the fastest way to move buyers through your marketing and sales funnels through the power of real-time conversations. It builds relationships and creates authentic experiences with customers and buyers. Drift and Community are great tools for marketers to implement this strategy, as they both empower human connection and authentic conversation.

CAMEO

Cameo is an American video-sharing website headquartered in Chicago. Cameo was created in 2016 by Steven Galanis, Martin Blencowe, and Devon Spinnler Townsend. The site allows celebrities to send personalized video messages to fans. To use this product in an empathetic way, find out who your audience or prospects really are fans of and use this tool to surprise them and make their day. It may be the cherry on top that makes them buy.

ACCOUNT-BASED MARKETING

Account-based marketing, also known as key account marketing, is a strategic approach to business marketing based on account awareness in which an organization considers and communicates with an individual prospect or customer accounts as markets of one. Imagine heading to a site and being greeted directly by your name, with some background on your current problems, and a solution tailored specifically to you. Yeah, I know, it's a *little* creepy, but it works.

GONG

Gong is a tool that created the Revenue Intelligence category to enable leading revenue teams to get the unfiltered truth about their customer interactions and their deals to transform the way they go to market. They do this by recording calls with customers/prospects and summarizing, tagging, and organizing the data so marketing, customer, and sales teams can execute on the insights taken *directly* from the source.

CHAPTER-6

NICE SALE! BUT, WE ARE JUST GETTING STARTED.

———

We are not thinking machines that feel, rather, we are feeling machines that think.

—ANTONIO DAMASIO, NEUROSCIENTIST

Take a moment to reflect on a recent purchase you made. What did you feel after you smashed the order button and committed to the product? That feeling is part of the post-purchase process, and it is arguably the most important phase of the buyer's journey. Why? It is your brand's opportunity to deliver on the brand promise that built trust with the buyer.

For me, recently I bought the latest and greatest version of the new iPhone to treat myself. I went through every phase of the buyer's journey confidently because Apple made me feel excited, curious, and, well, fancy. As I went through each phase of the buyer's journey, I was extremely excited to make this investment in myself, and I was confident I was going to *love* my new iPhone.

Right after I bought the iPhone, I had a serious case of buyer's remorse. Thoughts were whirling in my head. Do I really need to spend over a thousand dollars on a new phone? My phone works fine. What am I doing? Is this phone going to be too big? Will I get tired of the gold? Why did I buy the leather case? What a waste of money!

What solidified the purchase for me was the experience I had when receiving the product, remember the four P's of marketing: price, promotion, placement, and product. Marketing is not just one of these four P's; it is a combination of all of them, and Apple perfected each one. As I waited anxiously for the new iPhone to arrive, I received updates regularly on the status of my delivery (because Apple knows their price is high and creates anxiety). The brand also was sure to promote the ins and outs of my new product to help build positive anticipation rather than anxiety. To make sure my anxiety was calmed throughout my day, their placement of these messages was across all channels (email, text, and the Apple store app). Finally, the day came, and I received my product. Because Apple reassured me that I made the right decision to buy their product, I am now an absolute fan of my new iPhone. Not only am I a fan, I am an advocate and recommend the phone enthusiastically to anyone looking to buy a new phone.

BUYER AFFIRMATION

In my experience with Apple, I was treated with a great amount of empathy, and I started to wonder, who else embodies empathy in the post-purchase phase of the customer journey?

So, as one does, I went to Google. I searched the phrase "Empathy Marketing" daily and made it my goal to find a like-minded individual. As I scrounged through pages of search results, I became a bit discouraged. Not many people were talking about this concept, and I started wondering if it was just a hidden concept.

I set down my computer in frustration and picked up an old-fashioned hardcover book. At the time I was reading *The Context Marketing Revolution* by Mathew Sweezey. I flipped through the pages and there it was—empathy, on page 118. "Nobody cares about your brand. But they might begin to care, if you can prove you care about them. That's where empathy comes in, which is different than sympathy." Yes! That was exactly how I felt, so I contacted the author right away.

I told him about my thoughts on Empathy Marketing and how important it is. He emailed me back shortly after, agreed, and then asked, "Do you know Brian Carroll? He does a lot with empathy and is also a published author. He's also a good friend, and it would probably be good to chat with him about your idea. He's much deeper into that slice than I am."

Turns out, I am not the only one. I reached out to Carroll.

Carroll is the CEO and founder of markempa, a company that provides empathy-based marketing services so you can optimize your messaging to increase conversion and drive sales growth. Carroll's belief (and mine too) is that "all the automation tools, best practices, and data analytics won't help get better results until you master empathizing with your customers." With over eight thousand marketing technology companies in 2020, and counting, there is an abundance of possibility to understand consumer behavior (Brinker, 2020). This technology is so powerful and can help every business identify everything from traffic to customer journeys, trends to conversational marketing, and so much more.

What is all of this missing, though?

You guessed it, empathy.

When talking with Brian, he mentioned as a marketer, "You need to go beyond rational logic-based marketing to understand how your buyers feel." If you didn't believe in this already, 2020 was the perfect example. Across industries people were getting laid off, their anxieties doubled, they had to adjust to working from home, and so much more. If you didn't address this in your marketing, you were tone-deaf. In the midst of a global pandemic, your marketing strategy has to change to what your customers and future customers are feeling.

Oh, it also has to do that when we aren't in the midst of a global pandemic.

Using empathy to understand your different personas' emotions is the best way for you to build trust with your buyer pre- and post-purchase. If you are not only relevant with the times but hyper-relevant with how the times make your specific audience feel, you will win. Your audience and customers will know you care about the well-being of others and you aren't just focused on yourself. This will bring current customers back to buy more and bring customers on the fence to buy as well.

Buyer affirmation can look a lot like the story I told you about my iPhone, or it can look like companies taking a stand for their community. Either way, they are rooted in empathy. To be effective in the post-purchase phase of the customer journey, you have to be in tune with how your customers are feeling about the purchase and also the world.

Using empathy to understand your different personas' emotions is the best way for you to build trust with your buyer pre- and post-purchase. If you are not only relevant with the times but hyper-relevant with how the times make your specific audience feel, you will win. Your audience and customers will know you care about the well-being of others and you aren't just focused on yourself. This will bring current customers back to buy more and bring customers on the fence to buy as well.

COMMUNITY BUILDS EMPATHY

I wanted to know what type of marketer embodies empathy even more than a typical marketer. Who understands their audience on a much deeper, much more personal and community-based level? Then it hit me; let's go back to college.

Higher education marketers are faced with two sets of audiences: current and prospective students. These audiences (and, in some cases, their parents) are making quite the heavy investment into the institution higher education marketers work for, so it is important to maintain relationships full of trust and, you guessed it, empathy. Inside Higher Ed explains the importance of empathy in higher education by writing that "for higher education marketers, empathy might look like understanding how a seventeen- or eighteen-year-old must feel at this time as they are sheltering in place, disconnecting from social gatherings, graduating virtually, and thinking about a future that is unknown" (Weas, 2020).

For many marketing professionals, it may have been a few years or more since we were in the position of going to college. As we especially learned in 2020, a lot can change in just one year, so it is important for marketers to act with empathy in their messaging. *Forbes* brings up just one common problem new students face in their recent article "Building an Empathy Engine for Higher Education," saying "complicated paperwork requirements and lack of clarity around deadlines can often create unintended barriers to students' college-going aspirations. It may come as no surprise that this phenomenon is particularly acute among first-generation and low-income students, who are now at further risk of not attending school in the fall due to the disruptions caused by the COVID-19 crisis. Put simply, this will be an especially difficult summer for students who are already the most at-risk" (Magliozzi and Hurd, 2020).

Jon-Stephen Stansel ran social media at the University of Central Arkansas and has worked at Texas State University and the Texas Department of Transportation while consulting with many small businesses. In Stansel's work in higher education, he has learned a lot about what empathy means in a professional sense and how to use it. When I spoke to Stansel via Zoom from his home office, he mentioned that "social media marketers in general need to be social media users. I want to be clear on that because I don't mean they need to be influencers. They don't need to be tweeting about their jobs and business advice, but they need to understand what it's like to be on the other end of the platform. They need to have used social media to get customer service. They've got to understand the user experience on that platform. I think that's a requirement for empathy today." In order to build trust on any platform, you have to know what it is like to experience different emotions on that platform.

You have to meet your audience where they are. If they go to a certain platform to feel a specific emotion or resolve a specific emotion, you have to provide that.

From a report on trends in higher education marketing from the American Marketing Association, Tanya Pankratz, director of Brand and Creative Strategy at Collegis Education mentioned that "as major brands continue to create more unique, focused, and individualized consumer experiences, customized consumer experiences in higher education will no longer be a 'nice to have' but an expectation. It might already

You have to meet your audience where they are. If they go to a certain platform to feel a specific emotion or resolve a specific emotion, you have to provide that.

be an expectation for Millennials and Gen Z, since they've had customized experiences from their earliest shopping endeavors. Brands offering best-in-class moments—from awareness to conversion to advocacy—are winning the day and setting a high bar for the rest of the field" (American Marketing Association, 2020).

Stansel shares the unique perk that all higher education marketers have that other marketers don't—access to their audience in real life. "Understanding what the students want out of our social media marketing efforts sometimes just means sitting down with them and talking to them. Just one on one. I could be walking across campus and seeing what their issues are in real time. I like that for higher ed. I think that's an interesting position for a social media manager. If I ran social for Nike, which would be awesome, I would never see the people I interact with on a daily basis right there. I can take a walk across campus and say, 'Oh there's @kitty_john_78. She's having trouble registering for classes.' That's a nice kind of feeling that they're real people for me. They are not just social handles all the time. I think that's a good perspective to have for any marketer." This takes the concept of social listening to the next level, as he is social empathizing, processing, and acting on it. Not only is he focused on the emotions of his audience, Stansel is taking every opportunity he can to build community for his audience based on these emotions.

What if you don't have access to your customers or clients by strolling through the quad like Stansel does? Tapping into empathy might be just a phone call away. He recalls a moment when he was working at Texas State University in 2016. "In the United States there have been a lot of crises on campuses, or just anywhere. Shootings happen way too often. Some schools were putting out posts for every shooting that they had the schools in their thoughts and prayers. One day, my boss asked, 'What do we need to do?' and I said, 'I think we need to draw a line because we just can't post every time because it's happening every week.' It's not our role to say something every time something happens. And sure enough, a student was really upset that we didn't say anything about a shooting, and you know he reached out on social media and I called him.

"I had a one-on-one talk with them, and we both just really had a tough morning. We were talking about it, how it is an unfortunate time in our country, and more. If we're not doing something alongside it to back that action up, a social post doesn't mean much. Explaining that to the students was really helpful. I think that's beneficial."

In this process, Stansel did an amazing job at practicing empathy design thinking. He first identified the problem and empathized with the student, heard the students' feelings, described those feeling back to the student, and acted based on those feelings that inevitably built trust with that student for life.

These conversations are hard. Empathy is not easy. It takes work, emotional intelligence, and the ability to feel complicated emotions. Stansel embodies empathy in everything he does in his work, and his students notice it.

Even when I asked him what the most important aspect to empathy is, his answer was higher education. He believes that "educational experience, communal education, or different experiences are so important. I work at a university in a rural area, and I grew up in the rural South. I didn't have a lot of opportunities to meet people outside of growing up in Arkansas. It is very much a monoculture, and by going to university, being able to interact with people from not just across the country—being able to interact with people from all over the world—I was able to think differently and meet people with different backgrounds. People who came from different socioeconomic backgrounds and international students. This led to me understanding that there are other ways of living and thinking. This really helped me develop empathy. I think communal education and just breaking out of your own comfort zone is really important for developing empathy."

The main lesson I got from talking with Stansel is that you don't need to overcomplicate things when it comes to empathy. Yes, emotions are messy, difficult, and can be confusing, but understanding the emotions of your audience can be as simple as picking up the phone and calling them. Build that community.

EMPATHY = BUYER AFFIRMATION + COMMUNITY

Even after your customers buy your product, you must help them know they made the right choice. Affirm their decision with a balance of experience and community building.

PUT IT INTO ACTION

To meet your customers in an emotional and authentic way during their post-purchase phase, you can use the following strategies.

CUSTOMER RESEARCH

Just like market research, customer research is the action or activity of gathering information about consumers' needs and preferences, just with current customers. To ensure they are

The main lesson I got from talking with Stansel is that you don't need to overcomplicate things when it comes to empathy. Yes, emotions are messy, difficult, and can be confusing, but understanding the emotions of your audience can be as simple as picking up the phone and calling them. Build that community.

satisfied, always stay in touch with them, ask them for feedback, and make them feel heard.

STRONG CUSTOMER SUPPORT

When your customer needs you, you need to show up. According to HubSpot, 73 percent of customers say they stay loyal to brands because of friendly customer service reps. Make sure you are friendly, prompt, and solve their problems (Amaresan, 2021).

GONG

Gong was mentioned in the prior chapter as a purchase decision empathy tactic but also proves to be extremely beneficial for post-purchase. When your team is on calls with current customers, it is just as (or even more) important than prospects. The intel you can gather from current customers will help you create strong marketing, product, and customer retention strategies.

EMBRACING EMPATHY

Empathy in marketing is needed now more than ever. We are facing difficult times that can make people feel isolated, unheard, and unvalued. Our job as marketers is to solve problems for people with the products we market. Doing so in a more human way will only help make our world a better place to live. There are a ton of books out there about how you can sell better, influence better, negotiate better, etc. They all bring up valid points on decision science and psychology, but we must never forget we are extremely emotional creatures. As much as we think we are rational, we actually tend to be irrational most of the time.

When marketers are unable to embrace that fact, consumers get annoyed. They feel like they are just being sold to, getting a ton of spam in their email inbox, and they feel the need to avoid advertising at all costs. "About three-quarters of US internet users are concerned about how tech companies are using their data for commercial purposes, and only about one in ten are okay with that data being used for relevant ads, according to an April 2019 survey by the Internet Innovation Alliance (IIA) and CivicScience" (Perrin, 2019). People are fed up. They are tired. They don't want to be sold to. They want someone to solve their problems, tell them about it in a digestible way, and make it extremely easy to purchase it—all while providing a phenomenal, human, and empathetic brand experience along the way. Is that really too much to ask?

Not at all. In my time as a social media manager, I was fortunate to find a community on Twitter called #MarketingTwitter. Among our memes and virtual happy hours, we talk a lot about how we can improve marketing across our industries. This can look like conversations about digital accessibility, holding brands accountable, sharing intriguing new trends, ideas, and campaigns that have inspired us. The magic of #MarketingTwitter is that we are all the faces of the brands we work for. We all know the humans behind some of the largest cultural shifting brands in the world. Whether we run an account with one hundred followers or over one million followers, we leave our ego at the door and learn from each other. We celebrate each other. If I weren't in this community and did not learn about empathy at a young age, I would not be writing this book.

My mom always quoted Maya Angelou's famous saying, "I've learned that people will forget what you said, people will forget what you did, but people will never forget how you made them feel." In today's digital world, that could not be truer. We are constantly bombarded with noise, information, and marketing that it is near impossible to remember every message that you scroll past on social media. However, if they do it right, you remember what these brands make you feel.

I hope you are able to apply Empathy Marketing across the buyer's journey for whatever that looks like in your company, role, or industry. We have a lot of power as marketers. We play an instrumental role in the lives of our consumers. To make their lives better, we must apply Empathy Marketing.

As I talked with amazing marketers and influence professionals, I realized I was not alone in thinking about how to apply empathy in marketing. It seems simple, but as we get caught up in our day-to-day jobs, it can be easy for us to forget we are sending that email, social post, billboard, etc. to multiple people who may feel a certain way, and we are interrupting their day for our benefit. From the conversations outlined in this book and beyond, it is clear that marketers everywhere have to have a sense of empathy, understanding of emotion intelligence, and knowledge on how people make decisions. Many marketers claim that marketing is art plus science. In understanding your audience and providing value to them, that could not be truer. As mentioned throughout the book, empathy equals decision science (science) plus emotional intelligence (art).

I was surprised to see how marketers from various industries thought similarly about Empathy Marketing. They all argued that it is vital to provide value to customers across the entire journey. What also shocked me was how different each of these marketers were in the way they practice Empathy Marketing. Some used elaborate tools like social listening while others simply picked up the phone. Like anything that is an art plus science medium, you have to do what works best for you and your customers.

Ever since writing this book and discussing the topic of Empathy Marketing with people both inside and outside of the marketing industry, I've realized how many people crave empathy.

When there is so much noise on the internet, the media, etc., people can feel like they are drowning in conversations and are not heard when they want to be.

According to NPR, "More than three in five Americans are lonely, with more and more people reporting feeling like they are left out, poorly understood and lacking companionship, according to a new survey... Pervasive loneliness 'has widespread effects,' says Bert Uchino, a professor at the University of Utah who studies relationships and health. It's strongly linked to mental health issues such as anxiety and depression. It's an urgent time for the study of loneliness, Uchino adds. More and more research suggest that its impacts don't end with mental health. 'Evidence is really pointing to the fact that relationships—the kinds of bonds you have with people, how close you are, how connected you feel to others—impact physical health as well,' he says" (Renken, 2020). This loneliness fact is only increasing due to the state of our world, and the best thing we can do is to combat this with empathy. When people feel they are heard, understood, and taken care of, they feel less lonely.

Even by bringing up the topic of empathy and marketing to the world, I have felt less lonely. I am learning that sharing your ideas is scary, but if it is an idea that can make the world a better place, it is worth the risk. Writing this book was a challenge in multiple ways and taking time to face the challenge, share something new with the world, and believe in myself has allowed me to be more confident in my career and life.

At the beginning of this book, I mentioned that companies that understand how their brand plays a big role in the lives of their consumers from a psychological perspective and an entertainment perspective will win, by bringing humanity to their brand and showing deep passion for your customers. With that brand personality, they form connections that are meaningful to their audience. They build trust.

As marketing practitioners, our roles will only continue to get busier and more complicated as we try to stay on top of the next trends, technology, products, headlines, social media platforms, and more, but how we talk to our customers will make a brand build trust with their audience.

Because "people will forget what you did, but people will never forget how you made them feel," always make sure you make your audience *Feel Something*.

~~~~~~~

Throughout the book we learned a lot, but I want to highlight ten main principles to keep in mind when embracing empathy in your marketing strategy.

Here are the ten Empathy Marketing principles:

1. BE AUTHENTIC AND VULNERABLE

2. BE CONSTANTLY CURIOUS ABOUT YOUR AUDIENCE

3. TEST, TEST, TEST

4. BE HYPER-RELEVANT

5. ADVOCATE FOR YOUR AUDIENCE

6. DO THINGS THAT DON'T SCALE

7. TALK ABOUT THEM, NOT YOU

8. BE PROACTIVE NOT REACTIVE

9. IT IS NOT "YES AND"—IT IS YES, 100 PERCENT

10. CONSENT FOR COMMUNICATION

ACKNOWLEDGMENTS

I'd like to acknowledge the incredible professionals who shared their stories and brought *Feel Something* to life:

Daniel Pink, Santi Pochat, Brian Carrol, Christina Garnett, John Sabine, Jon-Stephen Stansel, Jake Bjorseth, Maya Malekian, Geneve Lau, Calum Shanlin, and more.

I'd also like to gratefully acknowledge:

Richard and Cynthia Timmons, Brendan and Katie Timmons, Elaine Sullivan, Fletcher and Courtney Ross, Susan and Stephen Sullivan, Jonathan Ross, Lockey Ross, Jonathan Mellin, Matthew Timmons, John and Patty Timmons, Thomas Timmons, Trey Holt, Rachel Reef-Simpson, Ann Wallin, Domm Holland, Jillian Guzzetti, Geralyn Sola, Nikhil Venkatesa, Vlad Magdalin, Danielle Babcock, Trent Brunngraber, Emry Rockenfield, Robert Vozzella, Richard Sola, Conor Biddle, Lindsey Young, Linda Johnson, Meu Morgan, Nayiri Nazarian, Bella Mumma, Katie Scannell, Carly Burgess, Natalia DeLucia, Brianna Hall, Anthony Sola, Matthew Tessier, Caroline Giercyk, The Shaughnessy Family, Jackie Kutil, Sarah Gardner, John Sabbey, Joshua Newman,

Philip Gaudette, Jess Ward, Tricia Sanchioni, Samantha Cosky, Emily Banas, Jessica McCormick, Janna Erickson, Samantha Sabanosh, Daniel Meyers, Ryan McDonald, Elise Rivera, Sean Collin, Kimberly Pfeifle, Allison Betito, Mark Kilens, Meg Button, Ashley Bird, Chelsea Castle, Christopher de Sa, Maria Corrin, Chris Degenaars, Alejandra Trujillo, Tim Ozmina, Kyle Wong, Daveen Fiant-Forehand, Paula Aciego, Jay Desai, Jon-Stephen Stansel, Theo Maroulis, Matthew Swain, Lucson Barthelemy, Mischa Vaughn, Juan Quintero, Suzie Hicks, Robin Shawver, Jack Nelson, Anne Vaeth, Casey Smith, Christine Johnson, Jenny Fowler, Evan McCrory, Christine Gritmon, Sara Ott, Joseph Yi, Liana Conway Price, Bria Riddick, Taylor Horen, Justin Hurdle, Chelsea Bradley, Bennett Boucher, Connor Skelly, Francisco Oller Garcia, Brittany Cabriales, Shaila Gupta, Jennifer Crim, Emily Park, Andrew L Rosch, Brett Rudy, Kerry-Ann Stimpson, Hillary Melin, Dan Holly, Melody Hendrickson, Randy Harrison, Lorraine Chon-Qui, Stephanie Stoops, Brandon Pare, Joel Primack, Michael Budd, Gauri Iyengar, Johann Warnholtz, Jemellee Santos, Richard King, John Sabine, Rey Sawan, June M Ritterbusch, Randy White, Jonathan Jacobs, Juliana Ocampo, Francisco Javier Buron Fernandez, Lucas Walker, Allison Betito, Shwathi Srinivasan, Felice M Magistrali, Lauren Kilberg,Bob Cargill, Francois Bourdeau, Bobbi Vanderhoof, David Curran, Lu Ann Reeb, Jason Meier, Jared Smith, Ian Simpson, Kristie Plantinga, Kimberly Vanderbeck, Katie Jane Parkes, Michael Fulwiler, Steve Lamar, Brendan Hufford, Pete Lorenco, Elissa Sanchez, Liam Barnes, Kelsea Little, Alyssa Powell, Jeremy Linaburg, Caiti Marlowe, Julie Dennehy, Nicole Ellingson, Eric Koester, Benjamin D Putano, Arielle Kimbarovsky, Anne Vaeth, Caroline Murray, Greg Rokisky, Jim MacLeod, Laura Tang, Diane Walter, Michael Hartford, Katherine Hale,

Natalie Clarke, Daniel Murray, Michaela L Mendes, Sarah Lemansky, Adrienne S Sheares, Marianne Sarazen Lonati, Hayley Fahey, Chantelle M, Nicole Tabak, Jordan Kirby, Jackie Wright, Evan Cohen, Alexis Rogers, Hunter O'Brien, Janet Mesh, Allen Gannett, Sean Wood, Adam Settlage, Kushaan Shah, Zibiao Chen, Angelic Vendette, Adam Ilenich, Cynthia Gleichauf, Christina Garnett, Rondene Grinam, Aaron Drill, Michelle Balaban, Jessi Sanfilippo, Amanda Natividad, Sam Chase, Santi Pochat, Bill King, Jamie Russo, Alexa Heinrich, Jayde Powell, Joseph Huber, Kiana Pirouz, and more.

Lastly, I'd like to acknowledge a few sources of inspiration:

Marty Neumeier, Robert Cialdini, Jeremy Rifkin, Kit Yarrow, Nadine Dietz, and more.

APPENDIX

INTRODUCTION:

Kemp, Simon. "WhatsApp Is the World's Favorite Social Platform (And Other Facts)." *Hootsuite (blog)*. April 22, 2021. https://blog.hootsuite.com/simon-kemp-social-media/.

Manning-Schaffel, Vivian. "What Is Empathy and How Do You Cultivate It?" *NBC News*, May 29, 2018. https://www.nbcnews.com/better/pop-culture/can-empathy-be-taught-ncna878211.

Silva, Clarissa. "Social Media's Impact on Self-Esteem." *HuffPost*, February 22, 2017. https://www.huffpost.com/entry/social-medias-impact-on-self-esteem_b_58ade038e4b0d818c4f0a4e4.

Tankovska, H. "Number of Social Network Users Worldwide from 2017 to 2025." January 28, 2021. *Statista*. https://www.statista.com/statistics/278414/number-of-worldwide-social-network-users/#:~:text=Social%20media%20usage%20is%20one,almost%204.41%20billion%20in%202025.

William, Craig "The Importance of Having a Mission-Driven Company." Forbes. May 15, 2018. https://www.forbes.com/ sites/williamcraig/2018/05/15/the-importance-of-having-a-mission-driven-company/?sh=75e532fe3a9c.

Zyoud, S.H., W.M Sweileh, R. Awang, et al. "Global Trends in Research Related to Social Media in Psychology: Mapping and Bibliometric Analysis," *Int J Ment Health Syst* 12, 4 (2018). https:// doi.org/10.1186/s13033-018-0182-6.

CHAPTER 1:

Buchanan, Leigh and Andrew O'Connell. "A Brief History of Decision Making." *Harvard Business Review (blog)*. January 2006. https://hbr.org/2006/01/a-brief-history-of-decision-making.

Harris, Tracey. *Successful Supervision and Leadership: Ensuring High-Performance Outcomes Using the PASE™ Model*. New York: Productivity Press, 2020.

Keim, Brandon. "Neanderthals Had Feelings, Too." *Wired*, October 5th, 2010. https://www.wired.com/2010/10/neanderthal-feelings/.

Krznaric, Roman. "Six Habits of Highly Empathic People." *Grater Good Magazine*, November 27, 2012. https://greatergood.berkeley.edu/article/item/six_habits_of_highly_empathic_people1#:~:text=The%20old%20view%20that%20we,social%20 cooperation%2C%20and%20mutual%20aid.

MediaKix. "8 Statistics Showing How Quickly COVID-19 Is Changing Social Media." *MediaKix (blog)*. Accessed June 6, 2021. https://mediakix.com/blog/covid-19-changing-social-media-statistics/.

Pew Research Center. "#BlackLivesMatter Surges on Twitter after George Floyd's Death." *FactTank (blog)*. Updated June 10, 2020. https://www.pewresearch.org/fact-tank/2020/06/10/blacklives-matter-surges-on-twitter-after-george-floyds-death/.

Ries, Julia. "Why Flu Cases are Down during a Massive Pandemic." *Healthline*, December 16, 2020. https://www.healthline.com/health-news/covid19-is-surging-but-flu-cases-are-down.

Smith, Jeremy Adam. "Can Patriotism Be Compassionate?" *Greater Good Magazine*, July 2, 2013. https://greatergood.berkeley.edu/article/item/can_patriotism_be_compassionate.

CHAPTER 2:

Cleveland Clinic. "3 Reasons You Crave Sweet or Salty Foods." *Health Essentials (blog)*. March 25, 2021. https://health.clevelandclinic.org/3-reasons-you-crave-sweet-or-salty-foods/.

Goleman, Daniel. "Hot to Help." *Greater Good Magazine*, March 1, 2008. https://greatergood.berkeley.edu/article/item/hot_to_help.

Karp, Myles. "WTF Happened to Government Cheese?" *Vice*, February 19, 2018. https://www.vice.com/en/article/wn7mgq/wtf-happened-to-government-cheese.

LinkedIn. "'My Company' Tab." Accessed December 2020. https://business.linkedin.com/marketing-solutions/my-company-tab.

Marty Neumeier. "Home." December 2020. https://www.martyneumeier.com/.

Miller, Carly. "Why Improv Comedy Is the Next Big Marketing Trend." *Contently (blog)*. March 26, 2016. https://contently. com/2016/05/26/why-improv-comedy-is-the-next-big-marketing-trend/.

Miller, Paul, dir. *In Living Color*. Season 3, episode 4, "Green Eggs and the Guvment Cheese." Aired October 13, 1991, on Fox. https://www.imdb.com/title/tt0098830/.

Parmar, Belinda. "The Most Empathetic Companies, 2016." *Harvard Business Review (blog)*. December 1, 2016. https://hbr. org/2016/12/the-most-and-least-empathetic-companies-2016.

Pink, Daniel. "Daniel Pink Teaches Sales and Persuasion." Masterclass. Accessed December 2020. https://www.masterclass.com/ classes/daniel-pink-teaches-sales-and-persuasion.

Ritchie, Josh. "8 Genius Examples of Empathetic Content Marketing in Action." *HubSpot (blog)*. October 9, 2017. https://blog.hubspot.com/marketing/empathetic-content-marketing-examples.

Schrader. Jessica. "Brené Brown on Empathy vs. Sympathy." *Psychology Today*. August 12, 2014. https://www.psychologytoday.com/ us/blog/partnering-in-mental-health/201408/bren-brown-empathy-vs-sympathy-0.

Velveeta Cheese. "NOT COOL CHRIS - WE DIDN'T SAY ANYTHING WHEN VISTA CAME OUT." Twitter. July 20, 2020. https://twitter.com/EatLiquidGold/status/1285309476799684608

Zelenski, Amy B., Norma Saldivar, Linda S. Park, Vonnie Schoenleber, Fauzia Osman, Sara Kraemer. "Interprofessional Improv:

Using Theater Techniques to Teach Health Professions Students Empathy in Teams." *Academic Medicine* Volume 95, Number 8. Abstract. https://www.ingentaconnect.com/content/wk/acm/2020/00000095/00000008/art00042.

CHAPTER 3:

Armstrong, Martin. "All of the Data Created in 2018 Is Equal To." *Statista.* April 16, 2019. https://www.statista.com/chart/17723/the-data-created-last-year-is-equal-to/.

Ebel, Grace. "Top 5 Gen Z Marketing Campaigns." *Khoros (blog).* July 30, 2019. https://khoros.com/blog/top-gen-z-campaigns.

Fraga, Juli. "'When I Was Your Age' And Other Pitfalls of Talking to Teens about Stress." *NPR (blog).* April 16, 2017. https://www.npr.org/sections/health-shots/2017/04/16/523592625/-when-i-was-your-age-and-other-conversational-pitfalls-of-talking-to-teens.

Google. "Our Mission." Accessed December 2020. https://www.google.com/search/howsearchworks/mission/#:~:text=Our%20company%20mission%20is%20to,a%20wide%20variety%20of%20sources.

Handley, Lucy. "There's a Generation below Millennials and Here's What They Want from Brands." *CNBC,* April 9, 2018. https://www.cnbc.com/2018/04/09/generation-z-what-they-want-from-brands-and-businesses.html.

IBM. "Move Over Millennials: Generation Z Is the Retail Industry's Next Big Buying Group." *Forbes,* July 12, 2017. https://www.forbes.com/sites/ibm/2017/01/12/move-over-millennials-generation-z-is-the-retail-industrys-next-big-buying-group/?sh=2d9c0b22f0a5.

Korn Ferry. "Age and Tenure in the C-Suite." *Korn Ferry (blog).* February 14, 2017. https://www.kornferry.com/about-us/press/age-and-tenure-in-the-c-suite-korn-ferry-institute-study-reveals-trends-by-title-and-industry#:~:text=The%20average%20age%20for%20a%20CEO%20across%20industries%20is%20058,CEO%20tenure%20is%208%20years.

Morning Consult. "Gen Z's Most Loved Brands." *Morning Consult (blog).* January 1 – February 28, 2019. https://morningconsult.com/most-loved-brands-genz/.

Netflix. "About." Accessed December 2020. https://about.netflix.com/en.

Prior, Ryan. "Acute Xnxiety: Internet Searches for Key Words Spiked to All-Time High Early in Pandemic." *CNN Health,* August 24th, 2020. https://www.cnn.com/2020/08/24/health/panic-attack-internet-search-coronavirus-trnd-wellness/index.html.

Rogers, Simon. "What Is Google Trends Data—and What Does It Mean?" *Google News Lab (blog).* July 1, 2016. https://medium.com/google-news-lab/what-is-google-trends-data-and-what-does-it-mean-b48f07342ee8.

TikTok. "About." Accessed December 2020. https://www.tiktok.com/about?lang=en.

Wiltshire, Emma. "Social Media Marketing Post-COVID: Marketers Predict the Future." *SocialMediaToday (blog).* July 16, 2020.

https://www.socialmediatoday.com/news/social-media-marketing-post-covid-marketers-predict-the-future/581779/.

YouTube. "About." Accessed December 2020. https://www.youtube.com/about/#:~:text=Our%20mission%20is%20to%20give,build%20community%20through%20our%20stories.

Zebra IQ. Gen Z Trends Report. *Zebra IQ*, 2020. https://zebraiq.com/report.

CHAPTER 4:

Alfonso III, Fernando. "Class-Action Lawsuit Filed against Robinhood Following Outrage over GameStop Stock Restriction." *CNN Business*, January 29, 2021. https://www.cnn.com/2021/01/28/investing/lawsuit-robinhood-gamestop-wallstreetbets/index.html.

Chi, Clifford. "How to Tell a Compelling Brand Story [Guide + Examples]." *HubSpot (blog)*. November 4, 2020. https://blog.hubspot.com/marketing/brand-story.

Li, Chushi. "Social Media Listening: An Essential Marketing Tool in 2021." *Socialbakers (blog)*. Socialbakers, 2021.https://www.socialbakers.com/blog/social-media-listening-report.

Twitter. "We're back. Our clearing firm, Apex, has resumed the ability to buy $GME, $AMC, and $KOSS on Public..." Twitter. January 28, 2021. https://twitter.com/public/status/1354877232762810370?lang=en.

Sprout Social. "Social Listening: Your Launchpad to Success on Social Media." *Sprout Social (blog)*. 2021. https://sproutsocial. com/social-listening/#social-listening-strategies.

Wise, Luan. "Empathy, Advocacy and Social Media: The Importance of Listening." *Global Marketing Alliance (blog)*. June 9th, 2017. https://www.the-gma.com/social-media-importance-listening.

CHAPTER 5:

Graham, Paul. "Do Things that Don't Scale." Accessed December 2020. http://paulgraham.com/ds.html.

Interaction Design Foundation. "What Is Design Thinking and Why Is It So Popular?" Accessed December 2020. https://www. interaction-design.org/literature/article/what-is-design-thinking-and-why-is-it-so-popular.

The Black Swan Group. "Chris Voss." Accessed December 2020. https://www.blackswanltd.com/our-team/chris-voss.

Voss, Chris. "Chris Voss Teaches the Art of Negotiation." Accessed December 2020. https://www.masterclass.com/classes/chris-voss-teaches-the-art-of-negotiation.

Watson, Imogen. "Ocean Spray Finally Reacts to Viral Skateboarding TikTok." *The Drum*, October 7, 2020. https://www. thedrum.com/news/2020/10/07/ocean-spray-finally-reacts-viral-skateboarding-tiktok?utm_campaign=Newsletter_Weekly_ Media&utm_source=pardot&utm_medium=email.

CHAPTER 6:

Amaresan, Swetha. "12 Data-Backed Reasons Customer Service Is Key to Business Growth." *HubSpot (blog)*. January 5, 2021. https://blog.hubspot.com/service/importance-customer-service.

American Marketing Association. "2020 Higher Ed Marketing Trends Roundup." *American Marketing Association (blog)*. January 14, 2020. https://www.ama.org/2020/01/14/2020-higher-ed-marketing-trends-roundup/.

Brinker, Scott. "Marketing Technology Landscape Supergraphic (2020): Martech 5000—Really 8,000, but Who's Counting?" *ChiefMarTec (blog)*. April 22, 2020. https://chiefmartec.com/2020/04/marketing-technology-landscape-2020-martech-5000/.

Magliozzi, Drew and Nicole Hurd. "Building an Empathy Engine for Higher Education." *Forbes,* May 11, 2020. https://www.forbes.com/sites/civicnation/2020/05/11/building-an-empathy-engine-for-higher-education/?sh=7c07042d1fa3.

Sweezey, Mathew. *Context Marketing Revolution: How to Motivate Buyers in the Age of Infinite Media.* Cambridge, MA: Harvard Business Review Press, March 24, 2020.

Weas, Patrick. "Reshaping Institutional Brand Value." *Inside Higher Ed (blog).* May 19, 2020. https://www.insidehighered.com/blogs/call-action-marketing-and-communications-higher-education/reshaping-institutional-brand-value.

CONCLUSION:

Perrin, Nicole. "Consumer Attitudes on Marketing 2019." *eMarketer (blog).* August 29, 2019. https://www.emarketer.com/content/consumer-attitudes-on-marketing-2019.

Renken, Elena. "Most Americans Are Lonely, and Our Workplace Culture May Not Be Helping." *NPR,* January 23, 2020. https://www.npr.org/sections/health-shots/2020/01/23/798676465/most-americans-are-lonely-and-our-workplace-culture-may-not-be-helping.

Made in United States
Orlando, FL
25 February 2022

15160314R00072